Smart Decisions

Wiley Series in
OPERATIONS RESEARCH AND MANAGEMENT SCIENCE

Founding Series Editor
James J. Cochran, University of Alabama

Operations Research and Management Science (ORMS) is a broad, interdisciplinary branch of applied mathematics concerned with improving the quality of decisions and processes and is a major component of the global modern movement towards the use of advanced analytics in industry and scientific research. The *Wiley Series in Operations Research and Management Science* features a broad collection of books that meet the varied needs of researchers, practitioners, policy makers, and students who use or need to improve their use of analytics. Reflecting the wide range of current research within the ORMS community, the Series encompasses application, methodology, and theory and provides coverage of both classical and cutting edge ORMS concepts and developments. Written by recognized international experts in the field, this collection is appropriate for students as well as professionals from private and public sectors including industry, government, and nonprofit organization who are interested in ORMS at a technical level. The Series is comprised of four sections: Analytics; Decision and Risk Analysis; Optimization Models; and Stochastic Models.

Smart Decisions

A Structured Approach to Decision Analysis Using MCDA

Dr. Richard Edgar Hodgett
University of Leeds
Leeds, UK

Dr. Sajid Siraj
University of Leeds
Leeds, UK

Dr. Ellen Louise Hogg
University of Leeds
Leeds, UK

Registered Office(s)
John Wiley & Sons, Inc., 111 River Street, Hoboken, NJ 07030, USA
John Wiley & Sons Ltd, The Atrium, Southern Gate, Chichester, West Sussex, PO19 8SQ, UK

For details of our global editorial offices, customer services, and more information about Wiley products visit us at www.wiley.com.

Wiley also publishes its books in a variety of electronic formats and by print-on-demand. Some content that appears in standard print versions of this book may not be available in other formats.

A catalogue record for this book is available from the Library of Congress

Hardback ISBN: 9781119309338; ePub ISBN: 9781119309321; ePDF ISBN: 9781119309352

Cover image: © sorbetto/Getty Images
Cover design by Wiley

Set in 9.5/12.5pt STIXTwo Text by Integra Software Services, Pondicherry, India

Printed and bound by CPI Group (UK) Ltd, Croydon, CR0 4YY

C9781119309338_160124

Contents

Preface

Decision-making is part of daily life, from choosing what to have for breakfast to choosing the places and route of your holiday next year. Most decisions are made through intuition without a second thought, but some decisions require a more structured approach as their outcomes could affect your life, your family's lives or the people you work with. The most important decisions in life require you to consider multiple criteria, objectives or goals to identify the best alternative(s) available to you. This is not straightforward as criteria, objectives and goals are often conflicting and have different levels of importance. Luckily, many different Multi-Criteria Decision Analysis (MCDA) methods have emerged to help rank, sort and evaluate decision problems. These methods have been discussed extensively in books and journal articles over the past 50 years but often in a way that is difficult to understand or implement in practice. Much of the content in this book originated in the authors' teaching material which has been very well received by current and former students on the MSc in Business Analytics and Decision Science program at Leeds University Business School. Many of our former students have gone on to use the methods in practice, helping many companies in different industries and sectors all around the world.

This book introduces the reader to several different MCDA approaches, explaining how they work and what unique features they have. It then presents step-by-step instructions of how to model a commonly faced decision such as choosing a car to purchase or selecting a school for your son or daughter to attend using Microsoft Excel and R. Naturally specialist software is available for the majority of MCDA methods, but software often gets superseded with new software and it doesn't teach you what's going on behind the buttons you press. Microsoft Excel is one of the most used spreadsheet software packages in business which has functionality for making calculations and producing graphical outputs – a perfect environment for modelling MCDA problems. That being said, modelling decisions in Microsoft Excel can take some time and when time is a constraint it's also nice to know how to quickly model a

MCDA problem in R. R is a free, open source programming language that has gained massively in popularity in recent years. It allows for the use of many external packages which includes the MCDA package for R that contains functionality for many popular MCDA methods. This means that you will only need to learn to use one software interface to quickly model most MCDA problems and will consequently learn to use one of the most popular[1] analytical programming languages and highly paid[2] IT skills today.

---

1 According to the IEEE, R was the 6th most popular programming language in 2020.
2 DICE named R as one of the highest-paying tech skills earning a salary of $126,249 in 2015.

Acknowledgements

The authors would like to thank the 'Centre for Decision Research (CDR) at Leeds University Business School (LUBS) for hiring three great members of staff to join their team of esteemed academics. There are so many wonderful people in CDR and at LUBS but the authors would like to specially thank Professor Barbara Summers and Professor Alan Pearman for their time, guidance and wisdom.

Dr Richard Hodgett would like to dedicate this book to his mother Susan, his father Stephen, his sister Sarah and his wonderful wife Louise for making him the man he is today. He would also like to make a special dedication to his wonderful daughter Sophie and son Thomas.

Dr Sajid Siraj would like to dedicate this book to his mother Zamurrad, his father Siraj, and his life partner Hina. He would also like to dedicate this work to his children Arham, Istafa and Abeeha, who fill his life with joy, fun, and sometimes misery.

Dr Louise Hogg would like to dedicate this book to her parents Lynn and Ian, sister Sarah, husband Richard and the most amazing children, Sophie and Tom.

1

Introduction

Welcome to Smart Decisions where you will learn about many ways to model and solve complex decision problems using Multi-Criteria Decision Analysis (MCDA). Each chapter will take you through a simple and common decision problem that most people face in their lifetimes, showing you how to solve it with a structured decision-making methodology in both Microsoft Excel and R. Microsoft Excel is the primary tool used in business and education for making spreadsheets and interactive formulaic templates while R is a popular tool used by specialists in analytics, data science and statistics. If you are not familiar with either Excel or R, don't worry! Chapter 2 is dedicated to telling you all about these software packages and how to use them. Trust me you will be an Excel and R whizz-kid in no time. That being said, this is not the primary aim of this book. The core of this book is to teach you about all of the wonderful and powerful decision-making methodologies out there which will help you justify and make better decisions at work and at home.

Let's start by discussing a hypothetical decision problem. Imagine you are a student who has just graduated and after years of partying and hard work you now have to decide what to do with your life. You are considering three distinct options; (1) find a job, (2) do further studies, or (3) start your own business. Your parents tell you to find a job related to your degree but your university professor suggests that you should do further studies before starting a professional career. To make matters more difficult, your friend, a recently established entrepreneur, has a great business idea and suggests you become a partner in their business. How do you decide what to do?

There are lots of interesting behavioural aspects to consider here, such as do you unconsciously favour the first option you discussed with your friend (this is referred to as anchoring) or do you prefer to stay in education as you haven't worked or started a business before (referred to as familiarity bias)? Although it is very important to acknowledge and understand the behavioural aspects of human decision-making, this will be rarely discussed in this book as the focus here is on the process of decision-making and not on the psychology of

Smart Decisions: A Structured Approach to Decision Analysis Using MCDA, First Edition.
Edited by Richard Edgar Hodgett, Sajid Siraj, and Ellen Louise Hogg.
© 2024 John Wiley & Sons Ltd. Published 2024 by John Wiley & Sons Ltd.

decision-making. That being said, it is important to understand both areas of decision-making and therefore if you want to read more about behavioural decision-making we recommend reading *Thinking Fast and Slow* by Daniel Kahneman, *Psychology of Judgment and Decision Making* by Scott Plous and *Preference, Belief, and Similarity* by Amos Tversky.

Most people who study decision-making now agree that there are two systems of decision-making, system 1 which is based on intuition or gut, and system 2 which is controlled, conscious and requires considerable effort (and time). We will be focusing on the methods and techniques that can be used for important and complex decisions that fit within system 2, or as we like to call it methods for structured decision-making.

Going back to the example we discussed about the recent graduate choosing what to do with their life. This is a particular problem where alternative options are already known to the decision-maker and the decision problem is to evaluate each of these options in order to select one of these alternatives based on several different criteria. This is referred to as an evaluation problem where the ultimate goal is to obtain a ranking or rating for each alternative. Other examples of such problems would be a regulatory authority wishing to publish the ranking of all universities in a country or a food agency seeking to rate all food shops from 1 (inadequate) to 5 (outstanding).

Another category of decision problems would be those where we search for a feasible solution which is not explicitly known to us. This category of problems can be labelled as design problems, for example, product pricing or time-tabling problems. A product can be priced with any value on a continuum but the decision-maker is interested in finding the most feasible price on this continuum. Similarly, one may find it difficult to manually schedule a timetable with no conflicts whatsoever, and therefore seek to find a feasible solution. In these two examples, the former one involves selection of a single value while the latter can be visualised as the selection of multiple values. The problems involving multiple values (sometimes called multivariate) can also be referred to as allocation problems. Table 1.1 summarises these categories of decision-making problems along with an example for each possible type of problems.

Table 1.1 Examples of evaluation and design decision problems.

	Evaluation	Design
Selection	Hiring a candidate	Product pricing
Ranking	Ranking universities	
Rating	Rating hotels	
Allocation	Allocate money and possessions in a will	Time-tabling classrooms

Another important categorisation is to consider the number of decision-makers. In the case of two or more decision-makers, conflicts may occur, usually due to different preferences, interests, or each person's level of knowledge. By contrast, those decisions involving a single decision-maker may not face these kinds of conflicts, although conflicts among different objectives/criteria may still occur, for example, searching to buy the cheapest house but wanting to live in a nice area.

1.1 How to Structure Your Decisions?

Whilst there can be many ways to structure a decision problem, Hammond J.S., Keeney R.L., and Raiffa H. (2002) proposed a very nice and simple framework known as PrOACT, which is an acronym for Problem, Objectives, Alternatives, Consequences, and Trade-offs.

Problem: The first element in this structure is the "Problem" itself. A good decision maker always questions the definition of the problem before identifying the ways to solve it. It is useless to find or suggest a wonderful solution to the wrong problem; therefore, it is important to identify the real problem before any further action.

Objective: After clearly identifying the real underlying problem, it is important to set objectives that can make us evaluate all the possible solutions. Some people may refer to these objectives as criteria. Linguistically, these two terms have slight difference, for example, a criterion can be "price", but the objective can be "finding cheapest price" or, if you are a rich person who wants to show off, the objective can be "finding the most expensive". In this example, both objectives are about the same price criterion, but one is trying to minimise while the other is trying to maximise. In most real-life problems, there are multiple criteria/objectives, and often these objectives are in conflict with each other. For example, one may dream of getting the cheapest item but with the highest quality.

Alternative: Consider a situation where there is only one possible course of action or choice. Will it be a decision problem? Not really, because the decision problem becomes a problem only when you have multiple alternative options, and you have to pick only one of these choices. Therefore, it is important to realise that identifying multiple alternative options is a very important step. One may miss a great (or best) solution without realising that it exists.

Consequences: After generating a good set of alternative options, it is important to evaluate the consequences of each of these alternatives. Usually this is done by creating a table where alternatives are placed in rows, objectives are places in columns, and then the consequences are penned down in each cell of this table. When describing the consequences in these cells, it is important to make sure they are as accurate as possible. Bad assessments will generate bad results, as they say "garbage in, garbage out".

Trade-offs: As we mentioned earlier, multiple objectives are often in conflict with each other, and therefore, you might end up with a table of consequences where there is no single clear winner. In this case, a trade-off analysis will be required where we need to sacrifice (or trade) something from one objective if we want to gain at least a little on another one.

In ProACT, there are three more elements that decision makers should consider in their decision-making exercise. These are Uncertainties, Risks, and Linked Decisions; but we will not discuss them here in detail. If you are interested in reading more about ProACT, we recommend reading the original book from Hammond J.S., Keeney R.L., and Raiffa H. (2002).

1.2   Different Stages in Decision-making

It is fair to say that every decision process starts with a need or desire to decide. The decision-maker realises this need when multiple alternatives appear viable to them whether known or unknown to them at the time of realisation. This realisation leads them to the two often-intertwined phases of structuring and exploration. For example, you have just moved to a new house and you realise you really need an air-conditioner. While exploring the various air-conditioning products on a popular shopping website, you make yourself aware of the criteria that must be taken into consideration when purchasing an air-conditioner. This is mostly true when the decision-maker has not taken a similar decision before. However, if the decision-maker is aware of taking similar decisions, it is likely they will have a decision structure in mind without needing to explore many options. For example, when buying lunch, you may consider the price, taste, travel time to get a particular food and the healthiness of the food. As you consider this decision very often in daily life you will already know many options available to you and the criteria that are important to you. This example is illustrated in Figure 1.1.

The two intertwined phases of exploration and structuring should give you enough information to construct a table of information, commonly referred to as a decision table where usually alternatives or options are listed as rows and the criteria as columns. A typical structure of a decision table is shown in Table 1.2. Some people prefer to format the decision table the other way around with criteria as rows and options as columns but in this book, we will stick to the format in Table 1.2.

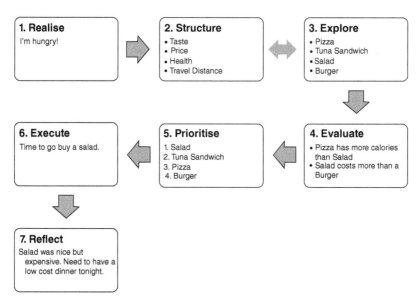

Figure 1.1 Steps in structured decision-making.

After the exploration and structuring phases, the next step in the decision-making process is the evaluation or assessment phase. Each cell in the decision table needs to be filled with information-bearing values. This information greatly varies from situation to situation. For example, in one situation it may be better to use a set of verbal values such as good, medium and bad for assessing each alternative with respect to each criterion. In a different situation, it may be better to look for factual values like battery life measured in years, engine capacity in horse power, product price or brand name. We included brand name here because factual values are not always quantitative and yet they bear information which may influence our decisions. Such non-numeric values will nevertheless need to be transformed into a quantitative value representing a

Table 1.2 The typical structure of a decision table.

	Criterion 1	Criterion 2	...	Criterion m
Alternative 1				
Alternative 2				
...				
Alternative n				

score for each alternative with respect to each criterion. For example, see Table 1.3 where the decision-maker has collected information about price, top speed, and brand for the three different cars they are interested in. The information about brand is purely categorical but he/she has assessed each brand to finally assign a percentage score representing their likeness for each brand.

Table 1.3 Example of preference elicitation.

	Price	Speed	Brand			Price	Speed	Brand
A	**£10k**	MEDIUM	Chipsy	→	A	**£10k**	70%	40%
B	£30k	**GOOD**	**Topsy**		B	£30k	**90%**	**80%**
C	£20k	BAD	Midsy		C	£20k	60%	60%

This process of converting raw information into quantitative scores is sometimes referred to as preference elicitation. Many decision analysts promote the use of direct ratings where the decision-maker is asked to assign a score between 0 and 100 to each alternative with respect to each criterion. We will discuss this in more detail in Chapter 3 with some practical examples. On the other hand, there is another school of thought which promotes the use of pairwise comparisons where a decision-maker has to make a number of one-to-one comparisons such as: do they prefer car A or car B in terms of Price and by how much? Some people say this way of decision-making is better as psychological theories suggest that the human mind can only focus on one comparison at a time. We will discuss this type of method in detail in Chapter 4 with some practical examples. Regardless of the method used for preference elicitation, the next obvious task is how to combine this information on different criteria in order to make (or aid) the final decision.

There are numerous methods which combine individual preference scores into an overall combined preference score (or a final ratings/ranking). One of the most straightforward and widely used approaches is the weighted sum method that is discussed in Chapter 4. As the name mentions, a weight is required for each criterion based on its importance, which is usually obtained by either the direct-rating or the pairwise comparison approach. Once the weights are obtained, the individual preference scores are aggregated using these weights.

Another class of aggregation methods are called ideal-point based methods. These methods create an imaginary ideal solution and in some cases an imaginary worst possible solution. The methods then attempt to quantify the distance of each alternative from the ideal or worst possible solutions. We will discuss this class of methods in Chapter 5.

All of the aggregation methods in Chapters 3–5 may need the individual preference scores in the decision table scaled appropriately before use. For example, you can't aggregate (or compare) preference scores ranging from 1 to 10 with preference scores ranging from 10 k to 100 k. For example, the price of cars in Table 1.3 may need to be converted into a 0-to-100 scale to overcome the problem of varied scales. This is achieved through a process called normalisation which is explained in Section 3.1 accompanied by a list of common techniques used for normalisation in Table 3.3.

Chapters 3–5 discuss the aggregation methods where overall scores are obtained by combining the individual preference scores. However, we often confront situations where someone vetoes against some of the alternatives. Another possibility is that some people may find minor differences to be insignificant. In such situations, it is difficult to use aggregation approaches. Another group of evaluation methods are outranking methods which, unlike the aggregation-based approaches, can still be used in these complicated situations with insignificance and vetoing. We will discuss outranking methods in Chapters 6 and 7.

In Chapter 8 we move on from evaluation methods to discuss methods for handling design problems where options are either infinite or unknown. These problems are mathematically modelled with an objective function (or multiple objective functions) along with a possible list of constraints that limit the possible range of solutions. This is discussed briefly in Section 2.2.9 then in more detail in Chapter 8. The goal of optimisation is to find a solution that maximises (or minimises) the value of an objective function without violating the constraints. There are situations in practice however where no solution can be found without violating the constraints. In such situations, the decision-maker may want to identify solutions that minimise these violations. In this respect, we will introduce Goal Programming in Chapter 8 where the constraints can be relaxed in order to find a feasible solution. The optimisation algorithm used in Chapter 8 is designed to work with problems that are represented with linear relationships. This method however will not work well with non-linear objective functions. To handle such non-linear problems, we will introduce the idea of evolutionary optimisation in Chapter 9 where we will show how Genetic Algorithms can be used to solve the travelling salesman problem. This is a practical problem of identifying a route between a number of different destinations that minimises distance or travelling time.

Throughout these chapters, we will introduce the problems with a decision table or objective function containing crisp quantitative values or equations – crisp meaning a precise number, not the snack food. However, we are often confronted with uncertainty in our data, be it the decision-makers assessments or the information we have captured from databases or other sources. In order to assess the robustness of solutions obtained from these methods, it is important to perform a sensitivity analysis which attempts to answer "what if?" types of questions. For example, what if the price of a particular car increases from £20 k to £22 k; will it still be the best alternative? Sensitivity analysis is a very important task to carry out post modelling a decision problem as it captures uncertainty in the obtained information.

This book will conclude with discussing this important topic of sensitivity analysis and will introduce a new technique called Simulated Uncertainty Range Evaluation (SURE) which has been practically applied in real-world applications.

References

"*Thinking Fast and Slow*" by Daniel Kahneman. Published 25 October 2011, publisher: Farrar, Straus and Giroux, New York, United States.
"*Psychology of Judgment and Decision Making*" by Scott Plous. Published 16 February 1993, publisher: McGraw-Hill Education, New York, United States.
"*Preference, Belief, and Similarity*" by Amos Tversky. Publication date: 16 December 2003, publisher: MIT Press, Massachusetts.
"Smart Choices: A Practical Guide to Making Better Decisions" by Howard Raiffa, John S. Hammond, and Ralph L. Keeney. Published 21 July 2015, publisher: Harvard Business Review Press, Brighton, Massachusetts.

2

Get Started with Excel and R

This chapter was designed to get you up to speed with the advanced features of Excel and to develop a solid understanding of R and how it can be used. If you are already a data whizz kid who knows all there is to know about Excel and R you may want to skip this chapter but as an expert you will know there is always plenty to learn about the two tools and even as an experienced user you may learn something new.

Unlike the following chapters in this book, this chapter will first introduce R and then progress onto Excel. The reason for this is that R comes with many example datasets built in. We will explore a dataset relating to cars in R and then extract it for use in Excel, being able to extract data from R will be useful for you when you want to do a quick decision analysis in R. So, let's get started!

2.1 Get Started with R

You may be asking yourself, what is R and why should I bother learning it? Well it's a free and open source programming language built with analytics in mind. It has become increasingly popular in recent years with the IEEE identifying it as the 6th most popular programming language in 2017, up from 9th position in 2014. Perhaps due to the increased popularity it has also recently been integrated into popular software and adapted in many ways. It was recently integrated into the most recent version of the SQL server (a database management system which powers the majority of online dynamic webpages) and packages have been developed to work directly with big data systems such as Apache Spark (a cluster computing framework popular in cloud computing applications). There are different versions of R which work on Windows, Linux, Mac and versions designed to run remotely on servers. The most popular programs to utilise R are the original R distribution from the CRAN repository (cran.r-project.org), R Studio (www.rstudio.com) and Microsoft R Open (mran. microsoft.com). R Studio has the advantage of an improved user interface and

Smart Decisions: A Structured Approach to Decision Analysis Using MCDA, First Edition.
Edited by Richard Edgar Hodgett, Sajid Siraj, and Ellen Louise Hogg.
© 2024 John Wiley & Sons Ltd. Published 2024 by John Wiley & Sons Ltd.

features for debugging while Microsoft R open is designed for parallel processing and has features for checkpoints. I would recommend learning to use R Studio as the improved interface makes many common operations much easier. The R Studio interface is divided up into four windows as shown in Figure 2.1.

The bottom left of the interface is the R console, which is common across all versions of R. In here you type commands and read/interpret the output. The top left window is used for writing R scripts. If this window isn't present when you first open R Studio, click on the File menu at the top and select New File then select R Script. The top right window displays your Environment and History. Your Environment lists all of the data you have imported and created while the History displays all of the previous commands you have entered. The bottom right window is used for working with files, viewing plots, working with external packages, viewing help documentation and viewing local web content. When working with files you need to be aware that R uses a working directory. This is a location where you store files you want to work with and where files will be created if you decide to save any of your data or results. You can change your R working directory by clicking on Tools at the menu at the top, selecting Global Options then under the General tab you can set your Default working directory. You can also do this in the console with the function setwd where if you entered setwd("C:\\") your R working directory would be set to the root directory of C: drive.

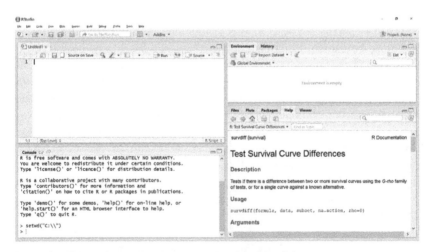

Figure 2.1 The R Studio User Interface. (copyright RStudio).

Working with R is quite straightforward. There are only a few things that you should know upfront, these are:

- R assigns information to variables (stores information) using an arrow written as <- instead of using an equal sign, for example: `num <- 20`. You can still use an equal sign (=) but it isn't the standard syntax and you may run into problems later.
- R is case sensitive, so if you set `num <- 20` you can't call it back as Num or NUM, it has to be num.
- Comments are written after a hash tag, so when you are writing code use a hash tag (#) to explain what it is you are doing. You will be thankful for all your comments when you come back to your code in a week/month/year's time!
- If you need help with a particular function you can use a question mark followed by the function name, for example `?setwd` will display the help information for the setwd function. You can also search the help system using two question marks, for example `??workingdirectory` will return information about the working directory.
- There are some special values which you will probably stumble upon such as NA which stands for Not Available and is a placeholder for a missing value, NULL which is an empty value, Inf which stands for infinity (e.g., 12/0) and NaN which stands for Not a Number (e.g,. 0/0).

2.1.1 Types of Data in R

Ok, let's start with some of the R basics and learn about the various different ways to store data. First a single variable. As discussed above you assign information to a single variable using an arrow, this information can be text or numerical. Try typing in and executing the following code below:

```
a <- "Hello World"    # save the text into a new variable
                      called a
a                     # Call back a
a <- 1204             # Set (overwrite) a as the number
                      1204
a/25                  # Divide a by 25 (not saving result)
b<-a/25               # Divide a by 25 and save this to
                      variable called b
a/b                   # Divide a by b
```

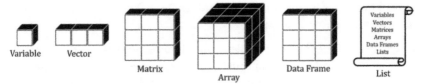

Figure 2.2 Types of data in R.

So, what if you need to store and use more information than one value? Well, R can store information in a variety of different ways as shown in Figure 2.2.

A vector is a combination or two or more variables and is very easy to create using the combine function which you can read about with ?c. Try the following code below to create a number of vectors with different types of information:

```
a <- c(1, 2, 3, 4, 5, 6, 7, 8, 9) # Create vector a –
                                     combine function c()
                                     is used.
a[3]              # Call the third element of vector a

b <- c("this", "is", "a", "vector", "of", "strings")
b[4]              # Call the fourth element of vector b
c <- c(T, F, T) # Create vector c with TRUE & FALSE
                  elements
c[2]              # Call the second element of vector c
d <- c(1:20)      # Use 1:20 instead of typing
                    1,2,3,4,5,6..20
d[5]              # Call the fifth element of vector d
```

A matrix allows you to store variables in two dimensions (rows and columns). You can easily create a matrix using the matrix function. First read about the matrix function using ?matrix then try the following code to create a number of matrices:

```
# Create matrix e with 5 rows and 4 columns
e <- matrix(1:20, nrow=5, ncol=4)

e          # Call back e to see what it looks like
           # Create matrix e with 4 rows and 5 columns
e <- matrix(1:20, nrow=4, ncol=5)

e          # Call back e to see what it looks like
```

```
e[1, 1]    # Call back the first row and first column of e
e[1, 4]    # Call back the first row and fourth column of e
e[4,]      # Call back the fourth row of e
e[,4]      # Call back the fourth column of e
f <- t(e)# Transpose (interchange row and column) e
?t         # Read about the transpose function t
```

An array allows you to store data in multiple dimensions and can be created in R using the array function. Read about the array function using ?array then try the following code below which shows how to create an array with three dimensions:

```
g <- array(1:24, c(4, 3, 2))  # Create array g of
                               dimensions 4, 3, 2.
g                              # Call back g to see what
                               it looks like
g <- array(1:24, c(2, 3, 4))  # Create array g of
                               dimensions 2, 3, 4.
g                              # Call back g to see what
                               it looks like
g[2, 3, 4]                     # Call back a specific
                               value from the array
```

Data frames are the most common way to store and manipulate data in R. You can think of a data frame like a table in a conventional database. The main difference between a data frame and the other data types we have discussed is that a data frame can store different formats of information. For example, a data frame can have columns that contain both numerical and textual information while a vector, matrix and array can only store one type of information. You can create a data frame of pre-existing information using the data.frame function (read about it using ?data.frame) as shown below:

```
studentID <- c(1, 2, 3, 4)
firstname <- c("Joe", "Susan", "Richard", "Sarah")
surname <- c("Bloggs", "Brown", "Smith", "White")
marks <- c(60, 67, 46, 73)
examdata <- data.frame(studentID, firstname, surname,
  marks)
```

You can call back information from a data frame in various different ways, for example the following code will all call back the marks column:

```
examdata[4]
examdata["marks"]
examdata$marks
```

A list is another way of combining and storing different formats of information. You can create lists of vectors, matrices, arrays, data frames and even lists. They are created using the list function (read about it using ?list) like follows:

```
h <- list (a = 1:5, b = "A String saying something", c
   = TRUE)
```

Calling back information from a list is quite simple, for example:

```
h[2]   # Call back second element in the list
h$b    # Call back element called b in the list
h$a[2] # Call back the second element in vector a in
         the list
```

2.1.2   Work with Data in R

Now that you are familiar with ways in which to store data in R, let's show you how to work with that data. Try the following code below which explores the mtcars dataset (a dataset included in R for testing purposes):

```
mtcars             # View all of the data in mtcars
head(mtcars, 5)    # View the first five rows of the
                     mtcars dataset
tail(mtcars, 5)    # View the last five rows of the
                     mtcars dataset
summary(mtcars)    # View summary of mtcars data
                   # Create a table of mpg against hp
table(mtcars$mpg,mtcars$hp)

        # Install an external package called dplyr for
        data pre-processing¹
install.packages("dplyr")

        # Add the dplyr package to your R library²
```

----

1 You only need to download and install a package once, unless there is an update you wish to install.

2 You will need to add a package you want to work with to your library every time you re-open R.

```
library("dplyr")
```

```
    # The filter function in the dplyr package can
    be used to select data that fits some particular
    criteria, e.g., the code below selects all cars
    which have four gears
filter(mtcars, gear == 4)
    # Filtering can be used with all standard
    logical operators³ and you can filter based on
    multiple criteria using & (AND) and | (OR)
filter(mtcars, gear == 3 | gear == 4)

filter(mtcars, gear == 3 & cyl == 6)

filter(mtcars, mpg > 21)
    # The select function in the dplyr package can
    be used to select or remove particular columns
    of information
select(mtcars, gear, mpg, hp) # select gear, mpg and
                                hp columns
select(mtcars, -drat)         # select all mtcars
                                columns without draft
                                column
    # The arrange function in the dplyr package can
    be used to order the rows of a dataset based on
    particular columns
arrange(mtcars, gear)       # arrange mtcars based on
                              gear column
arrange(mtcars, gear, mpg)  # arrange mtcars based on
                              gear then mpg
arrange(mtcars, desc(mpg))  # arrange using mpg in
                              descending order
    # The mutate function in the dplyr package can
    be used create new columns based on the
    information of pre-existing columns - the
```

---

3 I.e. greater than (>,) less than (<), greater or equal to (=>), less than or equal to (<=), not equal to (!=) and equal to (==).

example below creates mtcars with a new column called wt_mpg which is wt x mpg

```
mutate(mtcars, wt_mpg = wt * mpg)

mutate(mtcars, mpg_mean = mean(mpg), mpg_diff_mean =
  mpg - mpg_mean)

mutate(mtcars, mpg_mean_diff = mpg - mean(mpg))
    # The summarise function in the dplyr package
    can be used to summarise multiple values to a
    specified single value like the examples below
    which calculate the standard deviation (sd),
    median, mean, maximum (max) and minimum (min)
    values of particular columns

summarise(mtcars, sd(disp))

summarise(mtcars, median(mpg), mean(mpg), max(mpg),
  min(mpg))
```

The one final bit of R wizardry to share with you is how to use the piping operator. The piping operator looks strange but is very useful and allows you to write some complex operations with a very small amount of R code. The operator which looks like %>% simply can be read as the word then, for example:

```
mtcars%>%           # take the mtcars data frame, then..

group_by(gear) %>%  # group it by gear, then..

summarise(mean(mpg)) # calculate the mean mpg for each
                     gear type
```

That concludes the introductory lesson on R included in this book, if coding in R interests you then there are plenty of other books and online resources available which will help you build on what you have learnt. The last thing you need to do is export the mtcars dataset so we can work with it in Excel. To do this, set your working directory to the folder you want to save the file and then use: `write.csv(mtcars, file="mtcars.csv")`.

2.2 Get Started with Excel

Microsoft Excel is an application that is part of the Microsoft Office package for working with spreadsheets. It features many built-in functions for doing calculations, generating graphs, sorting and manipulating data.

There are many versions of Excel and this book will support 2007, 2010, 2013, 2016, 2011 for MacOSX and Office 365. Versions prior to this have a different user interface and reduced functionality. All screenshots contained in this book will be from the latest version of Excel in Office 365. If you are using a different version, you may need to explore the software to find a particular menu or setting as every version of excel has a slightly different layout.

In the last section, you exported the mtcars dataset from R as a CSV (Comma Separated Values) file to work with in Excel. You should now be able to open this file in Excel where you will see the data as shown in Figure 2.3. As CSV files can only store data without any Excel formatting, let's now save the data as an Excel (xlsx) file by clicking on **File** then **Save As** and selecting **Excel Workbook** from the **Save As Type** drop down menu as shown in Figure 2.4. You will now have an Excel data file open with the mtcars information. You can navigate the spreadsheet with your mouse scroll wheel, track pad or keyboard arrow keys.

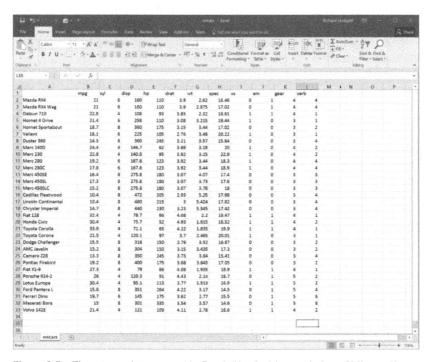

Figure 2.3 The mtcars data opened in Excel. (Used with permission of Microsoft).

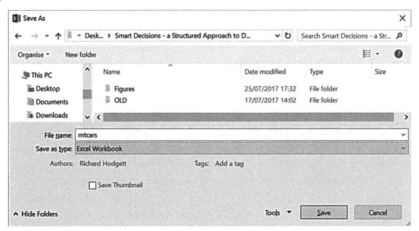

Figure 2.4   Save the mtcars data as an Excel Workbook.

2.2.1   Freeze Panes

When navigating through a much larger spreadsheet it is useful to lock the header row at the top so you can see what each column contains. To do this select the first line of the data (Mazda RX4), choose the View menu on the tabular menu and select Freeze Panes as shown in Figure 2.5.

To quickly navigate to the bottom row of the spreadsheet you can hold CTRL and press ↓ on your keyboard. Similarly, you can navigate to the top by holding CTRL and pressing ↑ on your keyboard.

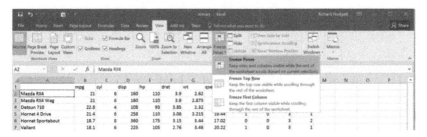

Figure 2.5   Select Freeze Panes from the View menu. (Used with permission of Microsoft).

2.2.2   Excel Formulas

One of the main features of Excel is that you can use formulas to make calculations with the values in select cells. To demonstrate this, we can calculate the average % MPG (miles per gallon) of all of the cars in the dataset.

Select cell B35 (B being the column and 35 being the row number) and in the Formula Bar type **=AVERAGE(B2:B33)** and press enter. The "B2:B33" is a shorter way of selecting all of the cells from B2 down to B33 inclusive rather than typing:

=AVERAGE(B2,B3,B4,B5,B6,B7,B8,B9,B10,B11,B12,B13,B14,B15,B16,B17, B18,B19,B20,B21,B22,B23,B24,B25,B26,B27,B28,B29,B30,B31,B32,B33)

This will calculate the average MPG (20.09) and place this into Cell B35.

There are many functions available in Excel. You can look up available Excel functions at the Microsoft Office webpage or in the Excel help menus.

2.2.3 Formatting Cells

The average MPG value calculated in B35 will display many numbers after the decimal place, depending on the width you have set the column. In most cases this is too much information. You can format the cell by right clicking on it and selecting format cells as shown in Figure 2.6.

You can then format this cell as a number with a specific number of digits after the decimal place, as shown in Figure 2.7. Within the format cells window, you can also modify the cell's alignment, font, border, colour etc.

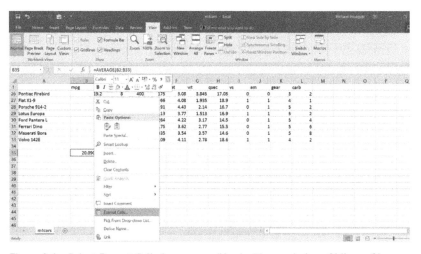

Figure 2.6 Select Format Cells from menu. (Used with permission of Microsoft).

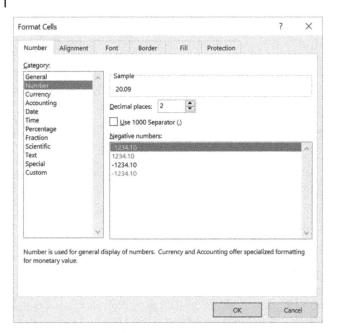

Figure 2.7 Set the cell as a number with two decimal places. (Used with permission of Microsoft).

2.2.4 Conditional Formatting

Sometimes you may want to update the cell format based on what value is in that particular cell. For example, if you owned a car showroom that stocked all of the cars listed in the mtcars dataset and you wanted to keep the total weight of all your car stock below 100 you could use conditional formatting to warn them if the value goes over this.

Start by adding the total weight of all of the cars in cell G35 with the formula

=SUM(G2:G33)

Then select cell G35 and click on the Conditional Formatting button on the home menu as shown in Figure 2.8.

There are a number of ways to use conditional formatting, but for this particular example we will simply create a new rule by clicking on the New Rule button. On the New Rule screen select "Format only cells that contain" and select that you want to format cells with a cell value greater than 100. Click the format button to change the properties of this formatted cell. As you will see in Figure 2.9, we have selected a red fill with white bold text.

When you click on OK you will see that the cell turns red as the value in the cell is more than 100. If you were to change the weight of the incredibly heavy Lincoln Continental from 5.424 to 2, you will see the total weight drops below

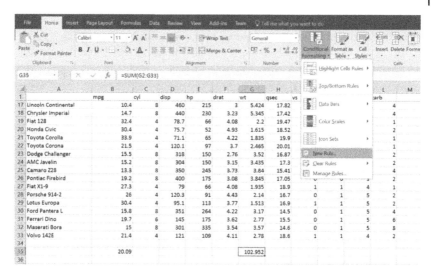

Figure 2.8 Add a new conditional formatting rule. (Used with permission of Microsoft).

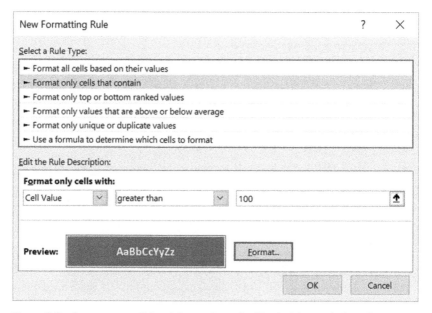

Figure 2.9 Set a new conditional formatting rule. (Used with permission of Microsoft).

100 and the cell G35 loses its red warning formatting. If you then return the Lincoln Continental weight back to 5.424 the red warning formatting returns. Cells can have more than one conditional formatting rule so you could add another conditional formatting rule to cell G35 so that it is green when the value is less than 100. You could even have three rules where its green when less than 95, yellow when it's between 95 and 100 and then red when over 100.

2.2.5   IF Statements

Another great tool in Excel is the ability to use a number of different IF statements. For example, the COUNTIF function allows you to identify how many cells conform to a particular rule.

For example, if you wanted to see how many of the cars listed have five gears you could place the following formula into cell K35:

=COUNTIF(K2:K33, 5)

You will see that there are five cars that have five gears. You can simply edit the formula in this cell and change the 5 to a 4 to see how many cars listed have four gears etc.

Instead, if you wanted to know the combined weight of all of the cars with five gears you could use SUMIF. Insert the following formula into cell K36:

=SUMIF(K2:K33, 5, G2:G33)

You will see that the five cars with five gears weigh a total of 13.16. You can also check multiple conditions using SUMIFS, so for example if you wanted to calculate the combined weight of all the cars in mtcars that have five gears and eight cylinders you could insert the following formula into cell K37:

=SUMIFS(G2:G33, C2:C33, 8, K2:K33, 5)

This gives you 6.74 which is calculated from the weights of the Maserati Bora (3.57) and Ford Pantera L (3.17) which both have eight cylinders and five gears.

You can also use the standard IF condition, so say if you wanted the average MPG of all of the cars in the mtcars dataset to be below 20 you could place the following formula in cell B36:

=IF(B35>20,"Average MPG is above 20","Average MPG is below 20")

As the average MPG in cell B35 is above 20, the cell in B36 will contain the message Average MPG is above 20.

2.2.6   Charts

Another one of the main features in Excel is the ability to generate charts using data very quickly. If you wanted to plot a graph of the average weight of all cars with a specific number of gears, first place the different number of gear options in cells N3:N5 as shown in Figure 2.10. Then in cell O3 place the following formula:

=AVERAGEIF($K$2:$K$33, N3, $G$2:$G$33)

This will show you the average weight of cars with three gears is 3.89. You will notice that the cell ranges K2:K33 and G2:G33 have been written as $K$2:$K$33 and $G$2:$G$33 respectively. This insures that when we replicate the formula in the other two cells that the selections remain constant, i.e. the $ stops the values changing. To illustrate this, select the bottom right corner of cell O3 and drag down to cell O5 as shown in Figure 2.11. This will then update cells O4 and O5 with the average weights of all cars with four and five gears. This happens because cell N3 in the formula in O3 is not constrained so when the cell is dragged down the cell number changes. Have a look at the formulas in O4 and O5 to see their respective formulas. Now let's generate a chart based on this information. Select cells O3 to O5 then click on the Insert tab and select 2D column chart as shown in Figure 2.12.

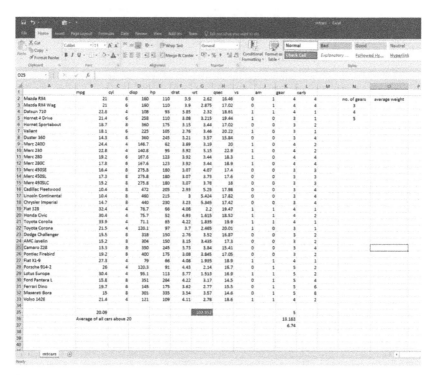

Figure 2.10 Add different gear options in cells N3:N5. (Used with permission of Microsoft).

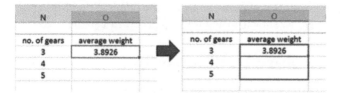

Figure 2.11 Drag from cell O3 to O5.

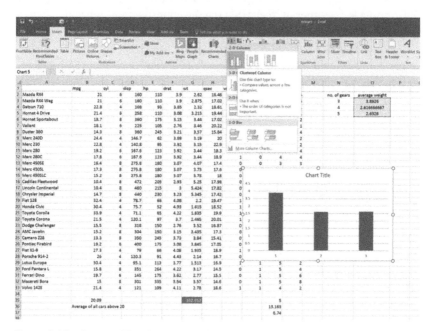

Figure 2.12 Create a 2D column chart. (Used with permission of Microsoft).

Next, we need to update the axis labels and chart title. To do this, click on the chart, then click on the axis to highlight them then right click and select **Select Data** as shown in Figure 2.13.

Now in the settings for the horizontal axis labels click on the **Edit** button and then select the axis label range of cells N3 to N5 as shown in Figure 2.14. Click **OK** then you will see the updated axis labels of 3, 4 and 5.

To change the chart title, you can simply double click on the title and amend the text so you end up with a chart that looks like Figure 2.15. Alternatively, you can click on the chart and select the Design tab where you will find options for amending the chart title, axes, legend, labels etc.

This example only showed how to create a 2D bar chart but there are many other different types of charts available in Excel that can be created in a similar way.

22.9	1	0	4	2
18.3	1	0	4	4
18.9	1	0	4	4
17.4	0	0	3	3
17.6	0			
18	0			
17.98	0			
17.82	0			
17.42	0			
19.47	1			
18.52	1			
19.9	1			
20.01	1			
16.87	0			
17.3	0			
15.41	0			
17.05	0			
18.9	1			
16.7	0			
16.9	1	1	5	2
14.5	0	1	5	4
15.5	0	1	5	6
14.6	0	1	5	8
18.6	1	1	4	2

5
13.163
6.74

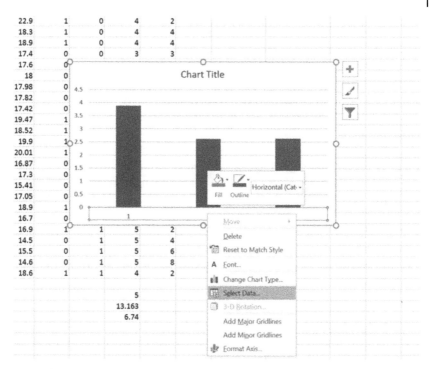

Figure 2.13   Select Axis data. (Used with permission of Microsoft).

Figure 2.14   Select Axis label range. (Used with permission of Microsoft).

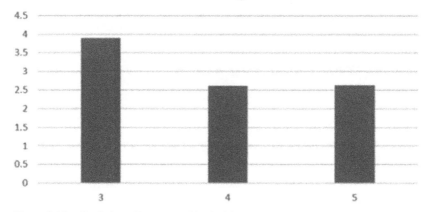

Figure 2.15   Final plot of bar chart. (Used with permission of Microsoft).

2.2.7 Searching and Sorting

There are various formulas in Excel to search for values or the location of values and functions for sorting. For example, if you wanted to compare how heavy the Dodge Challenger is compared with the rest of the cars in the mtcars dataset you can sort by weight and identify the rank of that car in the data set. To start, select all of the data and click on **Custom Sort** in the sort and filter button menu on the Home tab as shown in Figure 2.16.

Now choose to sort by wt on values in order of smallest to largest and click **OK**. This will then sort the data in order of weight, allowing you to find the rank of the Dodge Challenger. Instead of doing this manually you can also use a formula. In cell N26 enter:

$$=\text{MATCH(“Dodge Challenger”, A2:A33, 0)}$$

This will give you the result of 22, indicating that the Dodge Challenger is 22nd between the lightest car in 1st and the heaviest car in 32nd. You will notice that there is a 0 at the end of the MATCH formula. This sets MATCH

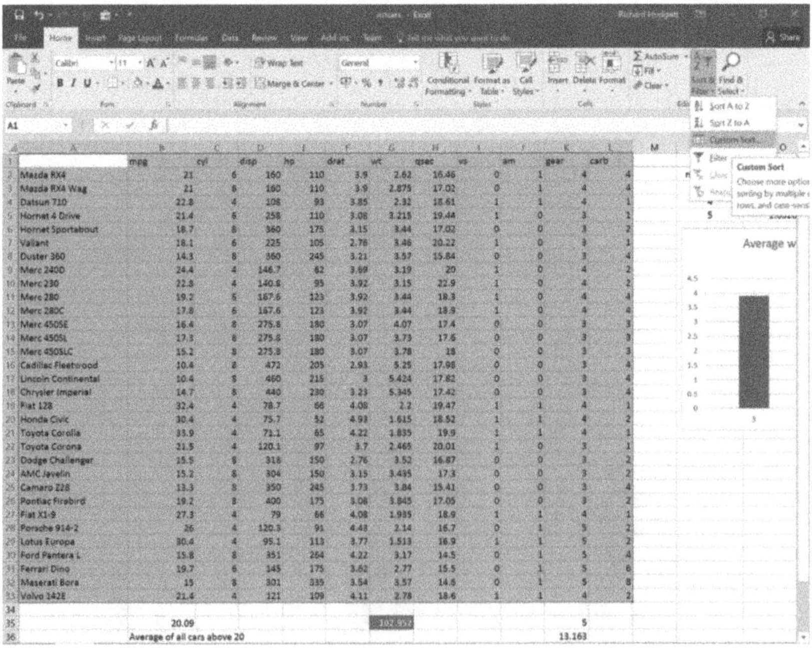

Figure 2.16 Select Custom Sort from the Sort & Filter menu. (Used with permission of Microsoft).

to search for the exact value of "Dodge Challenger". If you were searching cells containing numbers (rather than the name of a car), you could change this value to 1 for matching less than and –1 for matching greater than the value set.

To identify the 5th lightest car you could place the following formula into cell N27:

=INDEX(A2:A33, 5)

This will return Porsche 914-2. Another two formulas which can be used to find the rank of values are LARGE and SMALL. In the following cells insert the corresponding formulas:

Cell N28: **=LARGE(G2:G33, 3)**Cell N29: **=SMALL(G2:G33, 3)**

This will return the weight of the third heaviest car (5.25) and the third lightest car (1.835).

One of the most useful search functions in Excel is VLOOKUP. It can be used to search data for a particular item and return a value from a corresponding column. So, for example, you can search for how many gears a Dodge Challenger has by placing the following formula in cell N30:

=VLOOKUP("Dodge Challenger", A2:L33, 7, FALSE)

The 7 in the above formula indicates that you want to return data from the seventh column and the false indicates that you want an exact match rather than if you used true which would search for an approximate match. This formula correctly returns the weight of 3.52. The great thing about VLOOKUP is that you can search for words and phrases with partial information. For example, if you couldn't remember the car model name Challenger but you remembered that it started with a C you could search for "Dodge C*". Similarly, if you remembered Challenger but not the car brand then you could search for "*Challenger". You can also use the * in the middle of a word or phrase if you can't remember those particular characters. Even if you don't remember any of the characters but know the length of the word or phrase you can search for unknown characters with ?, e.g., "?????" would search for a five letter word.

The one limitation of VLOOKUP is that it cannot lookup values from columns on the left. One workaround for this is to use the OFFSET formula which can return information in a relative location to a particular cell. For example, if you spotted the car weight of 1.935 in cell G5 and you wanted to return the car's name, you could place the following formula in N31:

=OFFSET(G5, 0, -6)

In addition to VLOOKUP, there is also HLOOKUP which is used to search data for a particular item and return a value from a corresponding row rather than column.

2.2.8   Pivot Tables

Pivot tables in Excel are a great way to explore, display and summarise data. They can be used to quickly answer questions about your data. To create a Pivot table, select the data (A2:L33) and click on PivotTable from the insert tab as shown in Figure 2.17.

You can add the Pivot table to the existing worksheet but it is good practice to add it to a new worksheet as shown in Figure 2.18. Once you click **OK** you will see the new sheet with the Pivot table. You can then select the fields you

	mpg	cyl	disp	hp	drat	wt	qsec	vs	am	gear	carb
	30.4	4	95.1	113	3.77	1.513	16.9	1	1	5	2
	30.4	4	75.7	52	4.93	1.615	18.52	1	1	4	2
	33.9	4	71.1	65	4.22	1.835	19.9	1	1	4	1
	27.3	4	79	66	4.08	1.935	18.9	1	1	4	1
6 Porsche 914-2	26	4	120.3	91	4.43	2.14	16.7	0	1	5	2
7 Fiat 128	32.4	4	78.7	66	4.08	2.2	19.47	1	1	4	1
8 Datsun 710	22.8	4	108	93	3.85	2.32	18.61	1	1	4	1
9 Toyota Corona	21.5	4	120.1	97	3.7	2.465	20.01	1	0	3	1
10 Mazda RX4	21	6	160	110	3.9	2.62	16.46	0	1	4	4
11 Ferrari Dino	19.7	6	145	175	3.62	2.77	15.5	0	1	5	6
12 Volvo 142E	21.4	4	121	109	4.11	2.78	18.6	1	1	4	2
13 Mazda RX4 Wag	21	6	160	110	3.9	2.875	17.02	0	1	4	4
14 Merc 230	22.8	4	140.8	95	3.92	3.15	22.9	1	0	4	2
15 Ford Pantera L	15.8	8	351	264	4.22	3.17	14.5	0	1	5	4
16 Merc 240D	24.4	4	146.7	62	3.69	3.19	20	1	0	4	2
17 Hornet 4 Drive	21.4	6	258	110	3.08	3.215	19.44	1	0	3	1
18 AMC Javelin	15.2	8	304	150	3.15	3.435	17.3	0	0	3	2
19 Hornet Sportabout	18.7	8	360	175	3.15	3.44	17.02	0	0	3	2
20 Merc 280	19.2	6	167.6	123	3.92	3.44	18.3	1	0	4	4
21 Merc 280C	17.8	6	167.6	123	3.92	3.44	18.9	1	0	4	4
22 Valiant	18.1	6	225	105	2.76	3.46	20.22	1	0	3	1
23 Dodge Challenger	15.5	8	318	150	2.76	3.52	16.87	0	0	3	2
24 Duster 360	14.3	8	360	245	3.21	3.57	15.84	0	0	3	4
25 Maserati Bora	15	8	301	335	3.54	3.57	14.6	0	1	5	8
26 Merc 450SL	17.3	8	275.8	180	3.07	3.73	17.6	0	0	3	3
27 Merc 450SLC	15.2	8	275.8	180	3.07	3.78	18	0	0	3	3
28 Camaro Z28	13.3	8	350	245	3.73	3.84	15.41	0	0	3	4
29 Pontiac Firebird	19.2	8	400	175	3.08	3.845	17.05	0	0	3	2
30 Merc 450SE	16.4	8	275.8	180	3.07	4.07	17.4	0	0	3	3
31 Cadillac Fleetwood	10.4	8	472	205	2.93	5.25	17.98	0	0	3	4
32 Chrysler Imperial	14.7	8	440	230	3.23	5.345	17.42	0	0	3	4
33 Lincoln Continental	10.4	8	460	215	3	5.424	17.82	0	0	3	4

Figure 2.17   Select PivotTable from the Insert Menu. (Used with permission of Microsoft).

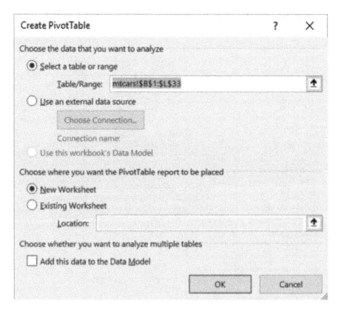

Figure 2.18   Create PivotTable in a new worksheet. (Used with permission of Microsoft).

want to work with in the field list located to the right side of the screen. You can experiment with Pivot tables by selecting different fields and dragging them between the sections at the bottom.

2.2.9   Excel Solver

Solver is built into Excel and provides functionality for optimisation. Optimisation is used to identify the best (or a good) combination of variables to minimise or maximise a particular function or problem.

In most cases solver is disabled when you first install Excel so you will need to enable it. To do this click on the **File** tab then click on the **Options** button on the left side of the screen. This will bring up an Options Menu with a number of tabs on the left. Click on the **Add-Ins** tab then at the bottom of the screen select Manage Excel Add-Ins and click Go as shown in Figure 2.19.

In the Add-Ins window, tick the "Solver Add-In" and click **OK**. This will add a Solver button to the Data tab in the main window in Excel as shown in Figure 2.20.

An example problem where you may use Solver is that you have a lorry that can transport the total weight of 10 and you want to transport as many cars as possible.

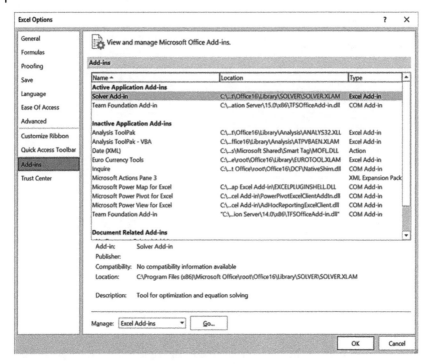

Figure 2.19   Find the menu to enable Excel Solver.

Figure 2.20   Solver added to the Data tab.

To identify the cars, create a new column by naming M1 "Number of Cars", add the label "Total Cars:" to L35 and "Total Weight:" to L36 so your worksheet looks like Figure 2.21.

Also place the following formulas in the following cells to count the number of cars and to add up the cars combined weights:

M35: **=SUM(M2:M33)** M36: **=SUMPRODUCT(M2:M33,G2:G33)**

Next, click on the data tab and then the solver button to bring up the solver parameters window. In here you need to set the objective function, which in this case is the number of total cars (cell M35). Click on the button and select the M35 cell. You want to identify the maximum number of cars to make sure that Max is selected.

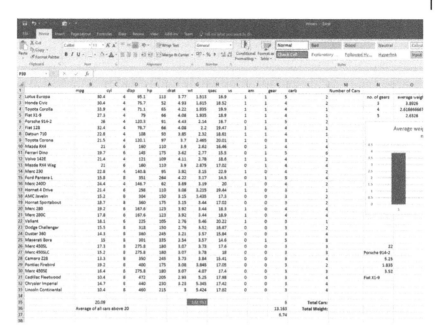

Figure 2.21 Formatted for solving problem. (Used with permission of Microsoft).

Figure 2.22 Add a Solver constraint. (Used with permission of Microsoft).

The changing variable cells are the cells showing the number of each car model in M2:M33. Click on the ▦ button and select these cells. Finally, you need to add the constraint of a maximum weight of 10. To do this, click on the **Add** button and set the cell reference to be the total weight cell (M36). Then select you want this value to be less than or equal to (<=) the constraint of 10 as shown in Figure 2.22. Click **OK** and check that the solving method is Simplex LP (which stands for Simplex Linear Programming) like in Figure 2.23 and click the **Solve** button.

A solution should be found almost immediately but what you will notice is that the solution doesn't make any sense as you cannot have 0.609 of a car. Therefore, you need to apply an integer constraint to the optimisation model.

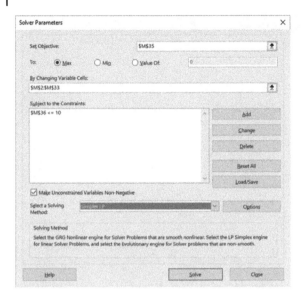

Figure 2.23 Solver Parameters settings for the problem. (Used with permission of Microsoft).

Figure 2.24 Add an integer constraint to the model. (Used with permission of Microsoft).

Re-open the solver parameters window from the button in the Data tab and then click to add a second constraint with the **Add** button. Set the cell reference to M2:M33 and in the middle drop-down box select **int** as shown in Figure 2.24.

Now click **OK** and then **Solve** again in the solver parameters window. This time solver will identify six cars (3 × Lotus Europa, 1 × Honda Civic and 2 × Toyota Corolla) which have a combined weight of 9.824, a little under the maximum weight of 10. Optimisation will be used and explained further in Chapters 8 and 9.

3

Direct Rating Methods

Direct rating methods are some of the simplest yet most effective ways to model a decision. Given a problem with no prior knowledge of decision modelling, most people would most likely try to tackle it using a form of a direct rating method. For example, let us consider assessing candidates shortlisted for a job where the company has decided to assess candidates based on their level of education, interview performance and previous work experience. A straightforward (and direct rating) approach would be to assign a score between 0 and 10 to each of the candidates with respect to the three criteria. For example, Adam is given 9 out of 10 for his top-class education as he has an MSc in Business Analytics and Decision Science from Leeds University Business School (taught by yours truly!). Similarly, Becky scores 8 in work experience as she has worked as a junior business analyst for two years in a competing firm. Charlie scores 6 for his poor performance at answering a technical question at the interview. In this way, we can construct a table of scores as shown in Table 3.1.

Getting graded out of 10 is an approach that we are all used to as is taking an average of multiple scores to obtain an overall score. In this example shown in Table 3.1, Becky is the best candidate with an average of 7 closely followed by Adam and Charlie. There are of course other ways to use direct ratings in addition to the 0–10 scale. Some people prefer verbal ratings (e.g., excellent, very good, good, average etc.) while others prefer a numeric scale from say 1 to 100.

If you choose to use a verbal scale, you must be able to translate the options into a numerical scale in order to aggregate them. One of the most widely used techniques adopted for this is the Simple Multi-Attribute Rating Technique (or simply SMART) which was developed by *Edwards*[1] in the

---

1 Edwards, W. (1977). How to use multi attribute utility measurement for social decision making. *IEEE Transactions on Systems, Man & Cybernetics* 7: 326–340.

Smart Decisions: A Structured Approach to Decision Analysis Using MCDA, First Edition.
Edited by Richard Edgar Hodgett, Sajid Siraj, and Ellen Louise Hogg.
© 2024 John Wiley & Sons Ltd. Published 2024 by John Wiley & Sons Ltd.

Table 3.1 A table of scores for interview candidates.

	Education	Interview	Experience	Average
Adam	**9**	7	4	**6**
Becky	6	7.5	8	7
Charlie	6	6	6	**6**

early 1970s. This is what we will use to model the example problem later in this chapter.

In Chapter 1 we discussed how a decision table is constructed with options as rows and criteria as columns as shown in Table 3.2. Each cell in the decision table needs to be assessed and filled with information-bearing values. A quantitative value is always needed to represent the score of each alternative with respect to each criterion. For this purpose, SMART proposes the use of scores between 0 and 100 for each alternative with respect to each criterion and then the weighted sum method is used to calculate a score which represents the performance of each alternative.

The weighted sum method is really simple, the score for each alternative (A_i) is just the sum product of each alternative score (a_{ij}) and criterion weight (w_j) as shown below:

$$A_i = \sum_j w_j a_{ij}$$

In this equation i identifies the alternative number and j identifies the criterion number in the decision table/matrix. If all criteria are assigned equal weights, then the weighted sum simply becomes a calculation of the average. In most decisions though there are always some criteria which are more important than others.

One point to consider with this method is that a low score in one criterion may get compensated by a higher score in another criterion. Therefore, this type of approach is sometimes referred to as a "compensation" approach.

Table 3.2 A template table of scores for SMART.

	Criterion 1	Criterion 2	...	Criterion m
Alternative 1				
Alternative 2				
...				
Alternative n				

3.1 Select a House Using a Direct Rating Method in Excel

Eddy has been working for three years as a web developer for a company based in Woodhouse (Leeds, UK). He rents an apartment with his partner who commutes to work in Dewsbury (a town roughly 10 miles south of Leeds) every day by train. Eddy and his partner want to buy their own property and have saved a deposit which would allow them to buy a property of value between £130,000 and £160,000. They started viewing properties which has helped them identify the important criteria on which they want to select a property to buy. Every time they visited a new property, they compared it to the properties they had already viewed and found out the pros and cons of those properties. Eddy categorised the criteria that mattered to them the most into two categories; external and internal. The external criteria included (1) the quality of the neighbourhood, (2) the commutability for himself and (3) for his partner, and (4) the distances from amenities like shops, parks and restaurants. The internal criteria included (1) the property purchase price, (2) the quality of construction, and (3) the facilities in the house like the number of bedrooms and total floor space.

After visiting many properties, Eddy and his partner shortlisted four which they really like but are quite different in their characteristics. One of the properties in Woodhouse would be great for Eddy's commutability and distances to amenities but the facilities in the house are poor as it has a small kitchen, has only one toilet and the heating system needs to be updated. Nonetheless, the quality of its construction is quite good with no signs of subsidence problems.

The second house is in Dewsbury, close to where Eddy's partner works. It has good facilities inside the property, the neighbourhood looks nice and the purchase price is less than the house in Woodhouse. However, the building has signs of damp and a leak from the shower has damaged the kitchen ceiling which could cause structural problems.

The third property is in Morley which is between where Eddy and his partner works. The house seems to be in a nice quiet area and is the cheapest of all the shortlisted properties. However, when researching trains Eddy identified that there is no direct train to Woodhouse so although his partner would be able to travel to work in less than ten minutes, his own travel time would be around one hour.

The final property is an apartment in Leeds city centre. It is the most expensive of the four properties but has direct train links to both Eddy and his partner's places of work. The apartment has been recently renovated to a high standard but the area is densely populated and suffers from some pollution due to heavy traffic.

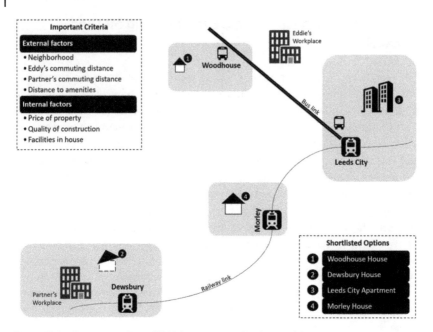

Figure 3.1 Representation of Eddy's property selection problem.

As you can see in Figure 3.1 all four options have their own unique advantages and disadvantages. Eddy and his partner were able to assign each property with a score between 0 and 100 for all of the external and internal criteria discussed earlier. Eddy was able to model this in Excel as shown in Figure 3.2. You can now open excel and create the table in the same cells as shown in Figure 3.2.

For the first time, Eddy and his partner felt as if they were able to visualise their difficult decision problem. Eddy stated exploring his decision table with conditional formatting to highlight higher (better) scores. He selected all of the scores (B3:H6), clicked **Conditional Formatting** in the Home tab then selected the **Green-White colour scale**. This option assigns darker shades of green to higher scores as shown in Figure 3.3.

Eddy quickly recognised that if he focuses on a single row at a time he can quickly assess that option. For example, when considering the Leeds City Apartment, he can see that it is not performing well in terms of Neighbourhood and Price criteria but is performing well in terms of the other criteria. Eddy also noticed that if he focuses on a single column, for example, the price criterion, it is easy to identify that the house in Morley is the best and the Leeds City Apartment is the worst.

Eddy wanted to quickly calculate the average score for each option, giving an equal weighting to each of the criteria. In cell J3, to the right of the decision table he entered: **=AVERAGE(B3:H3)**

	A	B	C	D	E	F	G	H	I
1		External Criteria				Internal Criteria			
2		Neighbourhood	EddyCommute	PartnerCommute	Distance Amenities	Price	Quality	Facilities	
3	Woodhouse House	60	100	30	80	60	70	20	
4	Dewsbury House	70	30	100	80	70	30	80	
5	Leeds City Apartment	30	80	80	100	20	80	100	
6	Morley House	90	30	90	50	100	60	70	
7									

Figure 3.2 Decision table for Eddy's property selection problem. (Used with permission of Microsoft).

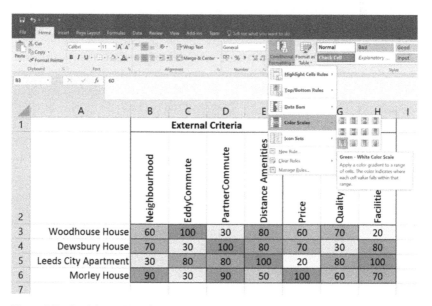

Figure 3.3 Decision table with conditional formatting. (Used with permission of Microsoft).

This calculates the average of the scores for the house in Woodhouse. He then dragged this cell down four places to calculate the average scores for all four properties. Finally, he added a Green – Yellow – Red conditional formatting rule to the four cells (J3:J6). The result (shown in Figure 3.4) shows that Leeds City Apartment and the house in Morley achieve the best score when all criteria are equal.

	A	B	C	D	E	F	G	H	I	J
1		External Criteria				Internal Criteria				
2		Neighbourhood	EddyCommute	PartnerCommute	Distance Amenities	Price	Quality	Facilities		Average
3	Woodhouse House	60	100	30	80	60	70	20		60.00
4	Dewsbury House	70	30	100	80	70	30	80		65.71
5	Leeds City Apartment	30	80	80	100	20	80	100		70.00
6	Morley House	90	30	90	50	100	60	70		70.00
7										

Figure 3.4 Decision table with average calculation. (Used with permission of Microsoft).

Eddy's partner found this result disappointing in a sense that their final choice was unclear due to a tie. Moreover, they found the apartment in Leeds City expensive leaving them without cash for any furnishing and decorations after moving. Therefore, Eddy added another row below the four properties and called it "Importance". He with his partner then quantified the level of importance for each of the criteria from 0 to 100. Since all of the criteria are somewhat important they did not give the score of 0 for any of the criteria. The scores given by Eddy and his partner are shown in Cells B8:H8 in Figure 3.5.

Eddy and his partner decided that price was of critical importance so they assigned the full score of 100. The criteria of neighbourhood, quality, and

	A	B	C	D	E	F	G	H	I
1		External Criteria				Internal Criteria			
2		Neighbourhood	EddyCommute	PartnerCommute	Distance Amenities	Price	Quality	Facilities	
3	Woodhouse House	60	100	30	80	60	70	20	
4	Dewsbury House	70	30	100	80	70	30	80	
5	Leeds City Apartment	30	80	80	100	20	80	100	
6	Morley House	90	30	90	50	100	60	70	
7									
8	Importance	80	50	80	50	100	80	80	
9	Relative Weights	15%	10%	15%	10%	19%	15%	15%	
10									

Figure 3.5 Decision table with criteria weights. (Used with permission of Microsoft).

facilities were of high importance after price so they agreed to assign 80 to all three. However, when it came to commutability, Eddy decided to compromise his comfort on his partner's comfort so they assigned 50 and 80 respectively. The distance to other amenities was considered less important so they assigned 50.

Figure 3.5 also shows a row for Relative weights, this is calculated by dividing the Importance (criteria weight) by the total amount of weight given. This is added by putting the following formula in Cell B9 and dragging the cell 6 cells to the right: **=B8/SUM($B$8:$H$8)**

Eddy then calculated the weighted sum score for each alternative by putting the following formula into Cell J3 and dragging the cell down by 3 cells: **=SUMPRODUCT(B3:H3, $B$9:$H$9)**

The SUMPRODUCT function calculates the sum of the products of two sets of values (i.e. the scores and criteria weights). For example, the weighted sum score for Woodhouse would be calculated by:

$$\left(60\times0.15\right)+\left(100\times0.1\right)+\left(30\times0.15\right)+\left(80\times0.1\right)+\left(60\times0.19\right)+\left(70\times0.15\right)+\left(20\times0.15\right)=56.54$$

The weighted sum results for all of the properties are shown in Figure 3.6. Now the situation looks quite different, the house in Morley turned out to be the highest scoring alternative.

Although the house in Morley turned out to be most feasible, Eddy and his partner couldn't resist changing the weights to investigate how it would change the outcome. To do this Eddy added interactive slider bars which can be used as levers to adjust and observe the weighted sum scores instantly. To

	A	B	C	D	E	F	G	H	I	J
1			External Criteria				Internal Criteria			
2		Neighbourhood	EddyCommute	PartnerCommute	Distance Amenities	Price	Quality	Facilities		Weighted Sum
3	Woodhouse House	60	100	30	80	60	70	20		56.54
4	Dewsbury House	70	30	100	80	70	30	80		67.12
5	Leeds City Apartment	30	80	80	100	20	80	100		65.77
6	Morley House	90	30	90	50	100	60	70		74.62
7										
8	Importance	80	50	80	50	100	80	80		
9	Relative Weights	15%	10%	15%	10%	19%	15%	15%		
10										

Figure 3.6 Weighted sum results. (Used with permission of Microsoft).

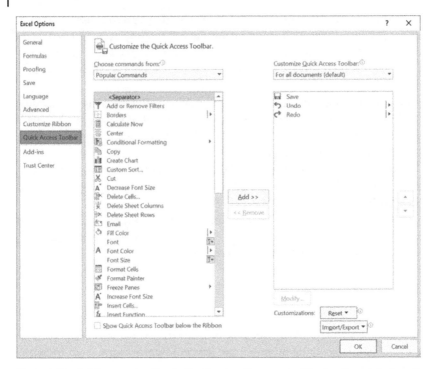

Figure 3.7 Quick access toolbar in the Excel options menu. (Used with permission of Microsoft).

do this Eddy clicked on the **File** menu and selected **Options**. In the Excel Options menu, he selected the **Quick Access Toolbar** tab (as shown in Figure 3.7).

He then selected **Developer** Tab from the drop-down menu and Added "Design Mode" and "Insert Controls" to the Quick Access Toolbar followed by clicking **OK**. This added two new menus to the top of the Excel interface. Eddy then inserted seven vertical scroll bars (as shown in Figure 3.8) and linked them to the importance scores in Cells B8:H8.

Once all the scroll bars were configured and linked as shown in Figure 3.9, Eddy and his partner found it very easy to adjust the weights by moving the levers up and down to see how the weighted sum scores are affected. This is commonly called a sensitivity analysis and is a very worthwhile process to test the sensitivity of a decision model.

After conducting a thorough sensitivity analysis, Eddy felt that the 0–100 scores used in SMART didn't fully represent the quantitative values he had for price, the two commute distances and the distance to amenities. He had the real values for these in the property brochures and from looking at

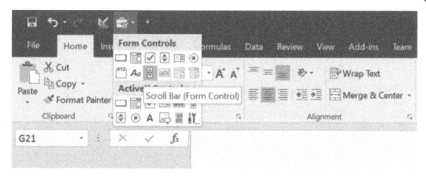

Figure 3.8 Add a vertical scroll bar from the form controls menu. (Used with permission of Microsoft).

	A	B	C	D	E	F	G	H	I	J
1			External Criteria				Internal Criteria			
2			Neighbourhood	EddyCommute	PartnerCommute	Distance Amenities	Price	Quality	Facilities		Weighted Sum
3	Woodhouse House		60	100	30	80	60	70	20		56.54
4	Dewsbury House		70	30	100	80	70	30	80		67.12
5	Leeds City Apartment		30	80	80	100	20	80	100		65.77
6	Morley House		90	30	90	50	100	60	70		74.62
7											
8	Importance		80	50	80	50	100	80	80		
9	Relative Weights		15%	10%	15%	10%	19%	15%	15%		
10											
11											

Figure 3.9 Weighted sum model with slider bars. (Used with permission of Microsoft).

online maps. In Cells L3:O6, Eddy entered the real values as shown in Figure 3.10.

Eddy realised when looking at the real values that they are all minimising (lower the better) while the weighted sum method can only handle maximising criteria (higher the better). Therefore, he decided to inverse the values for the minimising criterion. In Cell L8 he placed the following formula: **=L3^−1**

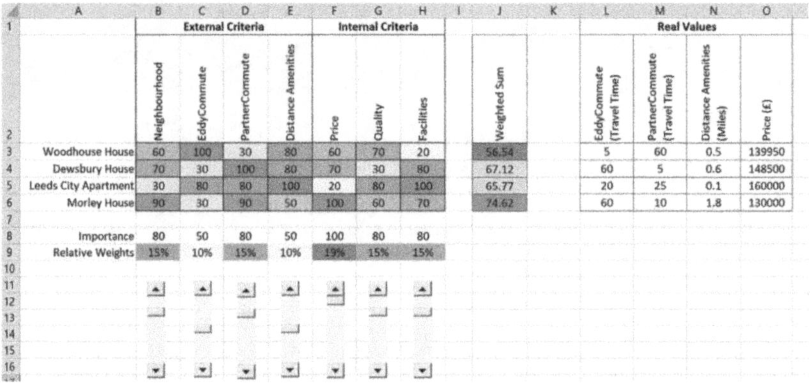

Figure 3.10 Real values entered for travel time, distance to amenities and property price. (Used with permission of Microsoft).

Figure 3.11 Real values have been inversed. (Used with permission of Microsoft).

He then dragged the cell down and to the right by 3 cells giving the values shown in Figure 3.11. You will notice that the lower values in cells L3:O6 are now the highest values in cells L8:O11.

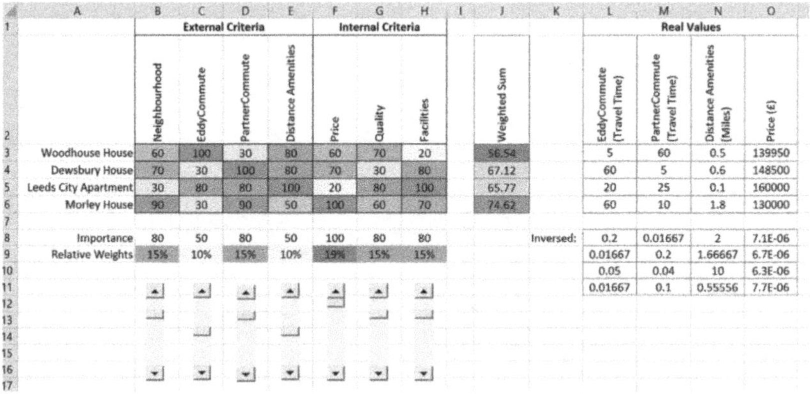

Eddy then noticed that the inversed values all varied greatly in proportion. This is because all of the values are measured with different units, i.e. time is measured in minutes between 5 and 60, distance is measured in miles between 0.1 and 1.8 and price is measured in pounds sterling between 130,000 and 160,000. These are of course very different to the 0–100 scale used previously.

To tackle this issue of different scales of measurement, Eddy decided to use normalisation to force all values to a similar scale. There are a few different ways to handle normalisation as shown in Table 3.3. Each method has its own advantages and limitations. Eddy selected to use summation ratio normalisation as it was the same way he had already handled the criteria weights.

Table 3.3 Common ways to handle normalisation

Name	Description	Equation
Summation Ratio Normalisation	Divide each value by the sum of all the values	$a_{ij}^* = \dfrac{a_{ij}}{\sum_{j=1}^{n} a_j}$
Vector Normalisation	Divide each value by the square root of the sum of all the values squared	$a_{ij}^* = \dfrac{a_{ij}}{\sqrt{\sum_{i=1}^{m} a_{ij}^2}}$
Max Scale Normalisation	Divide each value by the largest (max) value	$a_{ij}^* = \dfrac{a_{ij}}{a_j^{\max}}$
Max–Min Normalisation	Subtract the smallest (min) value then divide by the largest (max) minus the smallest (min) values	$a_{ij}^* = \dfrac{a_{ij} - a_j^{\min}}{a_j^{\max} - a_j^{\min}}$

where:

- a_{ij}^* is the normalised decision variable for the ith alternative with respect to the jth criterion.
- a_{ij} is the decision variable for the ith alternative with respect to the jth criterion.
- $a_j^{\max}$ is the largest decision variable with respect to the jth criterion.
- $a_j^{\min}$ is the smallest decision variable with respect to the jth criterion.

To do this he entered the following formula into cell L13:

$$= L8 / SUM\left(L\$8 : L\$11\right) * 100 \tag{7.2}$$

He then dragged the cell down and to the right by 3 cells. He then linked these values to the values in the table by placing the following formula into Cell C3 and dragging it down and to the right by 3 cells giving the values shown in Figure 3.12: **=L13**

	A	B Neighbourhood	C EddyCommute	D PartnerCommute	E Distance Amenities	F Price	G Quality	H Facilities	I	J Weighted Sum	K	L EddyCommute (Travel Time)	M PartnerCommute (Travel Time)	N Distance Amenities (Miles)	O Price (£)
			External Criteria				Internal Criteria						Real Values		
3	Woodhouse House	60	70.588	4.6729	14.063	25.683	70	20		36.87		5	60	0.5	139950
4	Dewsbury House	70	5.8824	56.075	11.719	24.204	30	80		42.67		60	5	0.6	148500
5	Leeds City Apartment	30	17.647	11.215	70.313	22.464	80	100		46.81		20	25	0.1	160000
6	Morley House	90	5.8824	28.037	3.9063	27.649	60	70		44.42		60	10	1.8	130000
7															
8	Importance	80	50	80	50	100	80	80	Inversed:			0.2	0.01667	2	7.1E-06
9	Relative Weights	15%	10%	15%	10%	19%	15%	15%				0.01667	0.2	1.66667	6.7E-06
10												0.05	0.04	10	6.3E-06
11												0.01667	0.1	0.55556	7.7E-06
12															
13											Normalised:	70.5882	4.6729	14.0625	25.6828
14												5.88235	56.0748	11.7188	24.2041
15												17.6471	11.215	70.3125	22.4645
16												5.88235	28.0374	3.90625	27.6486

Figure 3.12 Weighted sum model with real values. (Used with permission of Microsoft).

Eddy realised that with using the real values it made the Leeds City Apartment more attractive.

3.2 Select a House Using a Direct Rating Method in R

So, let's model the exact same decision problem in R. To start open R and run the following to install the MCDA package for R and add the package to your R library:

```
install.packages("MCDA")
library("MCDA")
```

You will now be able to use the weightedSum function in the MCDA package. Next, we need to enter the data. We can start by entering the criteria weights with the following:

```
criteriaWeights <- c(80, 50, 80, 50, 100, 80, 80)
names(criteriaWeights) <- c("Neighbourhood",
"EddyCommute", "PartnerCommute", "DistanceAmenities",
"Price", "Quality", "Facilities")
```

This creates a vector called criteriaWeights and names each criterion. We then should normalise the weights, this can be easily achieved using:

```
criteriaWeights <- criteriaWeights /
sum(criteriaWeights)
```

Next, we need to enter in the values in the decision table using the following:

```
Neighbourhood <- c(60, 70, 30, 90)
EddyCommute <- c(5, 60, 20, 60)
PartnerCommute <- c(60, 5, 25, 10)
DistanceAmenities <- c(0.5, 0.6, 0.1, 1.8)
Price <- c(139950, 148500, 160000, 130000)
Quality <- c(70, 30, 80, 60)
Facilities <- c(20, 80, 100, 70)
```

As we are using the real minimising values for EddyCommute, Partner Commute, DistanceAmenities and Price, we need to inverse the values using:

```
EddyCommute <- EddyCommute^-1
PartnerCommute <- PartnerCommute^-1
```

```
DistanceAmenities <- DistanceAmenities^-1
Price <- Price^-1
```

We then need to normalise them using:

```
EddyCommute <- EddyCommute / sum(EddyCommute) * 100
PartnerCommute <- PartnerCommute / sum(PartnerCommute)
* 100
DistanceAmenities <- DistanceAmenities /
sum(DistanceAmenities) * 100
Price <- Price / sum(Price) * 100
```

Finally, we can create our decision table (data frame) in R and name each of the columns (criteria) and rows (alternatives) using:

```
performanceTable <- data.frame(Neighbourhood,
EddyCommute, PartnerCommute, DistanceAmenities, Price,
Quality, Facilities)
row.names(performanceTable) <- c("Woodhouse
House","Dewsbury House","Leeds City Apartment","Morley
House")
colnames(performanceTable) <- c("Neighbourhood","Eddy
Commute","PartnerCommute","DistanceAmenities","Price",
"Quality","Facilities")
```

Now that all the data is entered, adjusted to maximising and normalised we can use the weightedSum function in the MCDA package for R to give us the results:

```
weightedSum(performanceTable, criteriaWeights)
```

As you will see the results in R are identical to what we found in Excel.

3.3 Further Problems to Test Your Direct Rating Method Skills

Now that you have mastered direct rating methods in Excel and R why don't you try to solve the following two problems. The solutions to the problems are available on our accompanying website: http://www.smartdecisionsbook.com

3.3.1 Purchase a New Laptop Using a Direct Rating Method

You have decided to purchase a new laptop and have identified three alternatives. You want to find the lowest cost laptop with the highest processing

Table 3.4 Decision table for laptop purchasing problem.

	Weight	Laptop 1	Laptop 2	Laptop 3
Purchase Price (£)	30%	319	299	399
Processing Power (Ghz)	25%	2.0	1.9	2.4
Number of Processing Cores	20%	4	2	2
Memory Size (Gb)	25%	8	4	16

power, the most number of processing cores and largest memory size. You have gathered all of this information and created a decision table as shown in Table 3.4. Using this information, decide which laptop you should purchase.

3.3.2 Select Manufacturing Equipment Using a Direct Rating Method

A games console manufacturer has approached you to help them decide on an injection moulding machine to purchase for the manufacture of the casing for their next generation product. They have found three possible machines to purchase and are interested in selecting the cheapest machine that will manufacture the most casings per hour with the best reliability. They have collected the data shown in Table 3.5. Using a direct weighting method recommend which injection moulding machine the company should purchase.

Table 3.5 Decision table for equipment selection problem.

	Weight	Machine 1	Machine 2	Machine 3
Purchase Price (£)	20%	50,000	42,000	65,000
Number of Casings per Hour	40%	500	380	720
Reliability (/10)	40%	7	8	6.5

4

Pairwise Comparison Methods

Do you consider yourself good at multi-tasking? Can you take a phone call while writing an email and keeping an eye on the TV? No me neither. Most people tend to focus on one task before turning their focus to another task. The idea of pairwise comparisons in decision-making is somewhat related to this school of thought. Instead of scoring each alternative with respect to each criterion like we did in the previous chapter, with pairwise comparisons we decompose a decision problem into several "head to head" comparisons. In this way, the decision-maker only has to focus on one comparison at a time, that is, which of the given two options is preferred and to what extent. For example, if you wish to rate three items A, B and C; a traditional direct rating approach would require you to assign a score of say 0 to 100 to each of these items. With pairwise comparisons we decompose this task into three smaller but simpler tasks, i.e., we compare A with B, then compare B with C, and finally compare A with C. Many people find this task much easier but I hear you thinking – how do we obtain our overall rankings from these pairwise comparisons? Is it similar to sports like football and rugby where teams play head to head matches and then each team gets an overall ranking based on their performance? Well, sort of. The answer is the Analytic Hierarchy Process (or AHP) which is the most widely-applied MCDA approach and the most distinguished pairwise comparison decision-making method. Before we get to how AHP calculates preferences, you should know that AHP considers problems using a hierarchical structure. Figure 4.1 illustrates this hierarchy where the ultimate goal (root) is at the top, followed by the criteria (nodes) and the alternatives placed at the bottom. You will notice from Figure 4.1 that alternatives are only assessed against the lowest level of criteria (criteria having no further sub-criteria such as C_{1-1} and C_{1-2} in Figure 4.1). The way AHP works is that the weights from lower hierarchies add up to elicit weights one level up in the hierarchy, and eventually end up giving overall weights at the root node level (i.e. the goal).

To use AHP, the decision-maker must be able to compare every pair of options and provide ordinal information (i.e. which option is more preferred) as well as cardinal information (i.e. how strong is the preference) as shown in Figure 4.2.

Smart Decisions: A Structured Approach to Decision Analysis Using MCDA, First Edition. Edited by Richard Edgar Hodgett, Sajid Siraj, and Ellen Louise Hogg.
© 2024 John Wiley & Sons Ltd. Published 2024 by John Wiley & Sons Ltd.

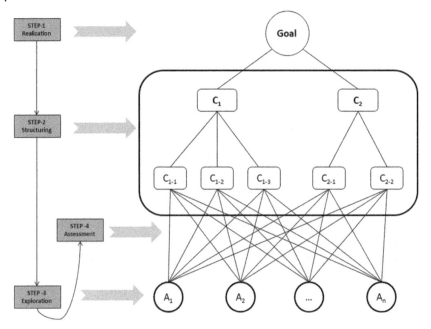

Figure 4.1 Overview of AHP hierarchy.

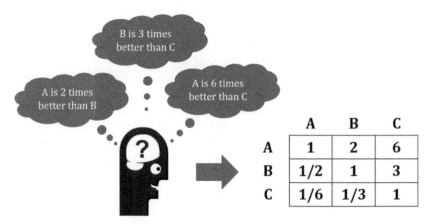

Figure 4.2 Overview of storing pairwise comparisons in a matrix.

Figure 4.2 also illustrates how pairwise comparisons can be stored in the format of a matrix or a table. You will notice that each option is listed vertically and horizontally and the value of 1 is placed diagonally throughout the matrix. This simply indicates that A is equal to A, B is equal to B and C is equal to C.

You will also notice that the values on one side of the matrix are the inverse of the values on the other side. For example, in the top-centre of the matrix, the 2 indicates that B is 2 times better than A which in return means A has to be ½ as good as B as shown in the middle-left of the matrix. This type of matrix is called a reciprocal matrix as it is symmetrically reciprocal as illustrated in Figure 4.3.

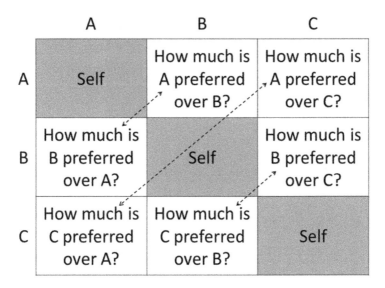

Figure 4.3 Pairwise comparison table showing its symmetrically reciprocal nature.

Now that you know how to collect and store pairwise comparisons, let's show you how to calculate the overall preference of each option. We will use the matrix values in Figure 4.2 as an example:

$$\begin{bmatrix} 1 & 2 & 6 \\ \frac{1}{2} & 1 & 3 \\ \frac{1}{6} & \frac{1}{3} & 1 \end{bmatrix}$$

There are a number of different ways to calculate the preference or ranking of each option but the most widely applied approaches are the eigenvector method or the geometric mean method. The eigenvector method requires you to calculate the principal eigenvector of the matrix. The principal eigenvector is a vector that represents the maximum amount of information that can be summarized in any single vector. The computation of this involves the use of high-order algebraic equations depending on the number of items to compare (n). As the high-order algebraic equations are not easy to compute, the easiest and quickest way is to estimate the principal eigenvector using the power method which is described in the steps below:

1) square the matrix;
2) sum the rows of the squared matrix and normalise these values;
3) repeat steps 1 and 2 until the difference between the normalised sums in two consecutive calculations are identical to a set number of decimal places (depending on how precise you want to be).

I know for an easy approach this seems quite difficult to understand and follow at first. Let's go through a quick example.

First, we convert the matrix from fractions to decimals:

$$\begin{bmatrix} 1 & 2 & 6 \\ \frac{1}{2} & 1 & 3 \\ \frac{1}{6} & \frac{1}{6} & 1 \end{bmatrix} \rightarrow \begin{bmatrix} 1 & 2 & 6 \\ 0.5 & 1 & 3 \\ 0.166^* & 0.333^* & 1 \end{bmatrix}$$

Then we need to square the matrix:

$$\begin{bmatrix} 1 & 2 & 6 \\ 0.5 & 1 & 3 \\ 0.166^* & 0.333^* & 1 \end{bmatrix} \times \begin{bmatrix} 1 & 2 & 6 \\ 0.5 & 1 & 3 \\ 0.166^* & 0.333^* & 1 \end{bmatrix} = \begin{bmatrix} 3 & 6 & 18 \\ 1.5 & 3 & 9 \\ 0.5 & 1 & 3 \end{bmatrix}$$

This is calculated by: $(1\times1)+(2\times0.5)+(6\times0.166^*)=3$
$(0.5\times1)+(1\times0.5)+(3\times0.166^*)=1.5$
$(0.166^*\times1)+(0.333^*\times0.5)+(0.166^*\times1)=0.5$
$(1\times2)+(2\times1)+(0.333^*\times6)=6$ etc.

Now we sum the rows and normalise to calculate the first estimation of our principal eigenvector:

$$\begin{bmatrix} 3 & 6 & 18 \\ 1.5 & 3 & 9 \\ 0.5 & 1 & 3 \end{bmatrix} \quad \begin{matrix} 27 \\ = 13.5 \\ 4.5 \end{matrix}$$

we then sum the row totals   27 / 45   **0.6**
$(27 + 13.5 + 4.5) = 45$ 13.5 / 45 = **0.3**
then divide each by the sum   4.5 / 45   **0.1**

This has placed a preference score of 0.6 for A, 0.3 for B and 0.1 for C. Normally you repeat this procedure to get a closer estimation of the principal eigenvector but we cheated a little and selected a problem which gives the final principal eigenvector in one iteration. I'm afraid we won't be so kind in the Excel example!

Using the geometric mean method is much simpler and is achieved from using the equation below:

$$r_i = \left(\prod_j a_{ij} \right)^{\frac{1}{n}}$$

where r_i are the preference scores, n is the number of items to compare and a_{ij} are the pairwise comparison values in the matrix.

So, using our example, the preference scores for A, B and C are calculated in two steps, the first step is to use the equation above:

$$A = (1 \times 2 \times 6)^{1/3} = 2.289428$$
$$B = (0.5 \times 1 \times 3)^{1/3} = 1.144714$$
$$C = \left(\frac{1}{6} \times \frac{1}{3} \times 1 \right)^{1/3} = 0.381571$$

The second step is to normalise the scores:

$$2.289428 + 1.144714 + 0.381571 = 3.815714$$
$$A = 2.289428 / 3.815714 = 0.6$$
$$B = 1.144714 / 3.815714 = 0.3$$
$$C = 0.381571 / 3.815714 = 0.1$$

As you will see the preference scores from using the geometric mean method are identical to the preference scores from the eigenvector method. This isn't always the case but they are usually very close as you will see in the example later.

One thing to consider with AHP and the use of pairwise comparisons is that the decision-maker can be inconsistent. For example, if a comic book nerd said they prefer superman over spiderman, spiderman over batman and batman over superman they are obviously being inconsistent (besides the fact that they are wrong as superman destroys both spiderman and batman). Comic book nerd or not, you want to avoid being inconsistent and luckily there is a way to gauge the level of inconsistency in judgments.

Professor Thomas Saaty, the inventor of AHP, proposed the use of the maximal eigenvalue (a value that relates to the principal eigenvector) to assess the level of inconsistency in pairwise comparisons. Using the fact that for a consistent matrix, the largest eigenvalue (λ_{max}) is equal to the size of the matrix (n), Saaty defined a measure of consistency referred to as the Consistency Index (CI), calculated by:

$$CI = \left(\lambda_{max} - n\right)/(n-1)$$

where perfect consistency implies that CI = 0 and CI > 0 for inconsistent matrices. To define a unique consistency measure which does not depend on the size of the matrix (i.e., n – the number of items to compare), Professor Saaty further introduced the idea of a Consistency Ratio (CR). This is the ratio between the CI and a Random Consistency Index (RCI) as shown:

CR=CI/RCI

In the above equation, RCI represents the average CI of randomly generated matrices of the same size (n). Table 4.1 shows the values usually used for RCI for matrix size (n) from 1 to 15.

If the CR value is smaller than or equal to 0.1 you can assume the pairwise matrix is consistent. When CR is larger than 0.1 the matrix is supposedly inconsistent and the advice is to revise the pairwise comparisons. However, it is up to you if you wish to revise your pairwise comparisons. It may not be necessary, especially your CR value is just above 0.1.

We'll show you in the R example below how to calculate CR.

Table 4.1 Values for RCI.

n	1	2	3	4	5	6	7	8	9	10	11	12	13	14	15
RCI	0	0	0.58	0.9	1.12	1.24	1.32	1.41	1.45	1.49	1.51	1.48	1.56	1.57	1.59

4.1 Select a Candidate to Hire Using AHP in Excel

ExcelsiOR is an analytical consultancy firm who wishes to hire a business analyst to join their team. The management recently finished interviewing four candidates that were shortlisted after a series of evaluations and assessments. They are finding it quite difficult to select one of the candidates as they all have a different blend of skills and appear to all to be equally experienced for the job. To solve this dilemma, they agreed to solve this problem using AHP.

They identified three criteria on which to select a candidate; analytical skills, people skills and experience. As ExcelsiOR are a consultancy firm, dealing with people and the ability to communicate complex analytics is very important.

Therefore, the management consider people skills twice as important as analytical skills and four times as important as experience. As the company has many experienced staff able to train and supervise inexperienced staff, they consider analytical stills to be three times as important as experience. This information allowed them to construct a pairwise matrix for their criteria weights as shown in Table 4.2.

To get started let's create a new Excel document and add five sheets named as in Figure 4.4 using the add sheet button and double clicking on the names to edit.

Then in the weights sheet, type in the criteria weights matrix from Table 4.2 as shown in Figure 4.5. Make sure for Cell C5 you enter the formula **=1/3** rather than the number.

Next, we need to square this matrix. Luckily, within Excel there is a feature that can return the matrix product of two arrays. We can use this to square the matrix in Figure 4.5. To insert an array formula, select cells C7:E9 and enter in the formula:

=MMULT(C3:E5,C3:E5)

Then rather than just pressing enter, press **CONTROL + SHIFT + ENTER** on the keyboard. This will insert the array formula for all selected cells giving the values shown in Figure 4.6.

Now we need to sum the rows and normalise the new matrix. Use the formula **=SUM(C7:E7)** in cell F7 and drag it down to cell F9. Then in cell F10 enter in the following formula: **=SUM(F7:F9)**

Table 4.2 Pairwise criteria weights for the candidate selection problem.

	Analytical Skills	People Skills	Experience
Analytical Skills	1	1/2	3
People Skills	2	1	4
Experience	1/3	1/4	1

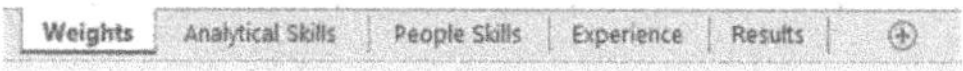

Figure 4.4 Names of the five Excel sheets.

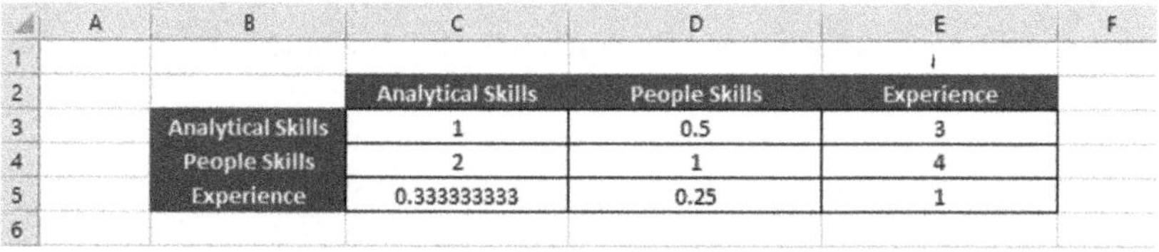

	A	B	C	D	E	F
1						
2			Analytical Skills	People Skills	Experience	
3		Analytical Skills	1	0.5	3	
4		People Skills	2	1	4	
5		Experience	0.333333333	0.25	1	
6						

Figure 4.5 Criteria weights entered into Excel. (Used with permission of Microsoft).

⊿	A	B	C	D	E	F
1						
2			Analytical Skills	People Skills	Experience	
3		Analytical Skills	1	0.5	3	
4		People Skills	2	1	4	
5		Experience	0.333333333	0.25	1	
6						
7			3	1.75	8	
8			5.333333333	3	14	
9			1.166666667	0.666666667	3	
10						

Figure 4.6 Squared criteria weights matrix using MMULT. (Used with permission of Microsoft).

⊿	A	B	C	D	E	F
1						
2			Analytical Skills	People Skills	Experience	
3		Analytical Skills	1	0.5	3	
4		People Skills	2	1	4	
5		Experience	0.333333333	0.25	1	
6						Summed Rows
7			3	1.75	8	12.75
8			5.333333333	3	14	22.33333333
9			1.166666667	0.666666667	3	4.833333333
10					Total:	39.91666667

Figure 4.7 Adding cell descriptions. (Used with permission of Microsoft).

At this point it is probably worthwhile formatting the cells and adding descriptions as shown in Figure 4.7. Next, to normalise the summed rows we need to divide each row sum by the summed rows total. In cell G7 insert the following formula: **=F7/$F$10**

Then drag the bottom right of cell G7 to G9. You can check the normalisation is correct by ensuring the sum of the normalised values is 1.

You will see the first estimation of the eigenvector is 0.319415 for analytical skills, 0.559499 for people skills and 0.121086 for experience. You now need to repeat this procedure until the estimations difference between the normalised sums in two consecutive calculations are identical to a set number of decimal places, let's say six decimal places. This will require repeating the procedure three more times as shown in Figure 4.8.

This gives the final weights of 0.319618 for analytical skills, 0.558425 for people skills and 0.121957 for experience which are identical to six decimal places in the last two iterations.

The next step is to apply the same procedure for each of the alternatives with respect to each of the criteria. The management at ExcelsiOR are trying to select one person from four potential candidates; Bob, Julie, Pete and Steve. They have compared each of the candidates against the three criteria and created the three pairwise comparison matrices in Table 4.3.

	A	B	C	D	E	F	G	H
1								
2			Analytical Skills	People Skills	Experience			
3		Analytical Skills	1	0.5	3			
4		People Skills	2	1	4			
5		Experience	0.333333333	0.25	1			
6						Summed Rows		
7			3	1.75	8	12.75	0.319415	
8			5.333333333	3	14	22.33333333	0.559499	
9			1.166666667	0.666666667	3	4.833333333	0.121086	
10					Total:	39.91666667		
11								
12			27.66666667	15.83333333	72.5	116	0.319620	
13			48.33333333	27.66666667	126.6666667	202.6666667	0.558417	
14			10.55555556	6.041666667	27.66666667	44.26388889	0.121962	
15					Total:	362.9305556		
16								
17			2296	1314.131944	6017.222222	9627.354167	0.319618	
18			4011.481481	2296	10513.05556	16820.53704	0.558425	
19			876.087963	501.4351852	2296	3673.523148	0.121957	
20					Total:	30121.41435		
21								
22			15814847.92	9051740.828	41446626.58	66313215.33	0.319618	
23			27631084.39	15814847.92	72413926.63	115859858.9	0.558425	
24			6034493.885	3453885.549	15814847.92	25303227.35	0.121957	
25					Total:	207476301.6		

Figure 4.8 Calculating weights to six decimal places. (Used with permission of Microsoft).

Table 4.3 Pairwise comparisons of candidates for the three criteria.

With respect to Analytical Skills:

	Bob	Julie	Pete	Steve
Bob	1	1/4	4	1/6
Julie	4	1	4	1/4
Pete	1/4	1/4	1	1/5
Steve	6	4	5	1

With respect to People Skills:

	Bob	Julie	Pete	Steve
Bob	1	2	5	1
Julie	1/2	1	3	2
Pete	1/5	1/3	1	1/4
Steve	1	1/2	4	1

With respect to Experience:

	Bob	Julie	Pete	Steve
Bob	1	1/3	1/5	1/2
Julie	3	1	1/2	2
Pete	5	2	1	3
Steve	2	1/2	1/3	1

In the Analytical Skills tab enter the matrix from Table 4.3 and repeat the same procedure that you used with the criteria weights.

You should get the values shown in Figure 4.9.

	A	B	C	D	E	F	G	H
1								
2			Bob	Julie	Pete	Steve		
3		Bob	1	0.25	4	0.16666667		
4		Julie	4	1	4	0.25		
5		Pete	0.25	0.25	1	0.2		
6		Steve	6	4	5	1		
7							Summed Rows	
8			4	2.166666667	9.833333333	1.195833333	17.19583333	0.106489
9			10.5	4	25.25	1.966666667	41.71666667	0.258341
10			2.7	1.3625	4	0.504166667	8.566666667	0.053051
11			29.25	10.75	50	4	94	0.582118
12						Total:	161.4791667	
13								
14			100.278125	43.58645833	193.1666667	18.78541667	355.8166667	0.116849
15			209.7	94.29479167	403.5833333	41.01979167	748.5979167	0.245836
16			50.653125	22.16979167	102.1614583	9.941666667	184.9260417	0.060729
17			481.875	217.5	959.0625	97.328125	1755.765625	0.576586
18						Total:	3045.10625	
19								
20			38032.50063	16849.03721	74711.73633	7420.421794	137013.696	0.115882
21			81011.10977	35900.75116	159134.0622	15811.92497	291857.8481	0.246844
22			19693.84346	8725.496956	38703.49699	3844.199235	70967.03664	0.060022
23			189410.7744	83943.4248	372184.541	36981.47095	682520.2112	0.577253
24						Total:	1182358.792	
25								
26			5688299385	2520496757	11176101635	1110257821	20495155599	0.115872
27			12118325038	5369654046	23809511772	2365287872	43662778728	0.246852
28			2946221671	1305476691	5788597222	575051624.2	10615347207	0.060015
29			28338548538	12556867596	55678241071	5531195694	1.02105E+11	0.577261
30						Total:	1.76878E+11	
31								
32			1.27291E+20	5.6403E+19	2.50096E+20	2.48451E+19	4.58635E+20	0.115872
33			2.71181E+20	1.20161E+20	5.32803E+20	5.29298E+19	9.77075E+20	0.246852
34			6.59298E+19	2.92136E+19	1.29536E+20	1.28684E+19	2.37548E+20	0.060015
35			6.34153E+20	2.80994E+20	1.24595E+21	1.23776E+20	2.28488E+21	0.577261
36						Total:	3.95813E+21	

Figure 4.9 Calculating Analytical Skills preferences to six decimal places. (Used with permission of Microsoft).

Repeat this procedure for People Skills and Experience using the matrices in Table 4.3. Your Excel sheets should resemble Figures 4.10 and 4.11.

Navigate to the Results sheet and enter in two blank tables as shown in Figure 4.12. Now we need to set the values within the tables to the corresponding values in the other respective sheets. You can do this one of two ways, for example:

1) Click on cell C3 and enter = then navigate to the Analytical Skills tab and select cell H32 (the final preference score for Bob) and hit enter.
2) Click on cell C3 and enter: =**'Analytical Skills'!H32**

	A	B	C	D	E	F	G	H
1								
2			Bob	Julie	Pete	Steve		
3		Bob	1	2	5	1		
4		Julie	0.5	1	3	2		
5		Pete	0.2	0.333333333	1	0.25		
6		Steve	1	0.5	4	1		
7							Summed Rows	
8			4	6.166666667	20	7.25	37.41666667	0.374073
9			3.6	4	16.5	5.25	29.35	0.293427
10			0.816666667	1.191666667	4	1.366666667	7.375	0.073732
11			3.05	4.333333333	14.5	4	25.88333333	0.258769
12						Total:	100.025	
13								
14			76.64583333	104.5833333	366.875	117.7083333	665.8125	0.378804
15			58.2875	80.6125	280.125	90.65	509.675	0.289972
16			14.99166667	20.49166667	71.8125	23.11041667	130.40625	0.074193
17			51.84166667	70.75416667	248.5	80.67916667	451.775	0.257031
18						Total:	1757.66875	
19								
20			23572.7487	32292.83594	113012.5781	36477.57682	205355.7396	0.378607
21			18065.18281	24748.36953	86608.80469	27955.81953	157378.1766	0.290152
22			4618.128385	6326.479036	22140.26953	7146.359635	40231.23659	0.074173
23			16005.50286	21926.01094	76733.60156	24768.12786	139433.2432	0.257068
24						Total:	542398.396	
25								
26			2244799021	3075205398	10762045810	3473759259	19555809488	0.378607
27			1720347363	2356746171	8247712584	2662186025	14986992143	0.290153
28			439778667	602463613.9	2108392830	680544316.9	3831179428	0.074173
29			1524183058	2088015863	7307259017	2358627636	13278085574	0.257068
30						Total:	51652066634	
31								
32			2.03571E+19	2.78877E+19	9.75963E+19	3.1502E+19	1.77343E+20	0.378607
33			1.56011E+19	2.13723E+19	7.47949E+19	2.41422E+19	1.35911E+20	0.290153
34			3.98816E+18	5.46348E+18	1.91201E+19	6.17156E+18	3.47433E+19	0.074173
35			1.38222E+19	1.89353E+19	6.62664E+19	2.13894E+19	1.20413E+20	0.257068
36						Total:	4.6841E+20	
37								

Figure 4.10 Calculating People Skills preferences to six decimal places. (Used with permission of Microsoft).

Either way this will update cell C3 with the preference score for Bob with respect to Analytical Skills. You can now drag this cell down by three places to retrieve the values for Julie, Pete and Steve. Repeat this for People Skills and Experience. Use the same process for the criteria weights so you end up with two complete tables as shown in Figure 4.13.

Now we can simply work out the results using the weighted sum method (discussed in Chapter 3) by placing the following formula in cell H3:

=SUMPRODUCT(C3:E3,$C$8:$E$8)

This calculates the overall AHP score for Bob by finding the sum product of the weights and his scores for each of the criteria. As the weight cells are constrained you can drag this cell down three places to see the final AHP scores for all of the candidates. As you can see in Figure 4.14, Steve is the best candidate, followed by Julie, Bob then Pete.

	A	B	C	D	E	F	G	H
1								
2			Bob	Julie	Pete	Steve		
3		Bob	1.00	0.33	0.20	0.50		
4		Julie	3.00	1.00	0.50	2.00		
5		Pete	5.00	2.00	1.00	3.00		
6		Steve	2.00	0.50	0.33	1.00		
7							Summed Rows	
8			4	1.316666667	0.733333333	2.266666667	8.316666667	0.087945
9			12.5	4	2.266666667	7	25.76666667	0.272471
10			22	7.166666667	4	12.5	45.66666667	0.482904
11			7.166666667	2.333333333	1.316666667	4	14.81666667	0.156680
12						Total:	94.56666667	
13								
14			64.83611111	21.07777778	11.83555556	36.51666667	134.2661111	0.088151
15			200.0333333	65.03611111	36.51666667	112.6666667	414.2527778	0.271973
16			355.1666667	115.4666667	64.83611111	200.0333333	735.5027778	0.482886
17			115.4666667	37.53888889	21.07777778	65.03611111	239.1194444	0.156991
18						Total:	1523.141111	
19								
20			16840.03204	5474.82508	3074.12316	9484.769241	34873.74953	0.088150
21			51957.52074	16891.79316	9484.769241	29263.90481	107597.988	0.271974
22			92249.61537	29991.06574	16840.03204	51957.52074	191038.2339	0.482886
23			29991.06574	9750.328179	5474.82508	16891.79316	62108.01216	0.156990
24						Total:	395617.9835	
25								
26			1136090034	369351685.2	207391570.1	639877156	2352710445	0.088150
27			3505244015	1139582027	639877156	1974249843	7258953041	0.271974
28			6223495798	2023306774	1136090034	3505244015	12888136621	0.482886
29			2023306774	657792731.4	369351685.2	1139582027	4190033217	0.156990
30						Total:	26689833325	
31								

Figure 4.11 Calculating Experience preferences to six decimal places. (Used with permission of Microsoft).

	A	B	C	D	E
1					
2			Analytical Skills	People Skills	Experience
3		Bob			
4		Julie			
5		Pete			
6		Steve			
7					
8		Weights:			
9					

Figure 4.12 Format of the results sheet. (Used with permission of Microsoft).

	A	B	C	D	E
1					
2			Analytical Skills	People Skills	Experience
3		Bob	0.115872	0.378607	0.088150
4		Julie	0.246852	0.290153	0.271974
5		Pete	0.060015	0.074173	0.482886
6		Steve	0.577261	0.257068	0.156990
7					
8		Weights:	0.319618	0.558425	0.121957
9					

Figure 4.13 Complete tables in the Results tab. (Used with permission of Microsoft).

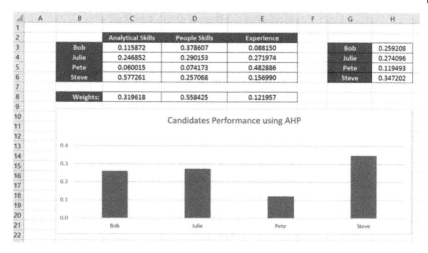

Figure 4.14 Results of the AHP analysis in Excel. (Used with permission of Microsoft).

I bet you are tired of using the MMULT function by now? Using the eigenvector method in Excel is longwinded but at least you now know the process. Using the geometric mean method is much quicker thanks to the GEOMEAN function. We will quickly show you how to use it.

In the Weights tab select cell F3 and enter:

=GEOMEAN(C3:E3)

Drag this cell down by three places. Now in cell G3 enter:

=F3/SUM($F$3:$F$5)

Drag this cell down by three places and that's it!

If you repeat this process in the Analytical Skills, People Skills and Experience tabs you can then create new tables in the Results tab to calculate AHP scores using the geometric mean method. As you will see in Figure 4.15 the results using geometric mean are not exactly the same but are very similar to those using the eigenvector method shown in Figure 4.14.

	Analytical Skills	People Skills	Experience			
Bob	0.112149	0.383013	0.088218		Bob	0.260488
Julie	0.248226	0.283462	0.271717		Julie	0.270767
Pete	0.058689	0.077388	0.483189		Pete	0.120902
Steve	0.580936	0.256137	0.156876		Steve	0.347843
Weights:	0.319618	0.558425	0.121957			

Figure 4.15 Results of the AHP analysis using geometric mean in Excel. (Used with permission of Microsoft).

4.2 Select a Candidate to Hire Using AHP in R

So, let's show you how easy it is to model the exact same decision problem in R. To start open R and run the following to install the MCDA package for R and add the package to your R library:

```
install.packages("MCDA")
library("MCDA")
```

We will be using the AHP function in the MCDA package but first we need to input our data. Let's start by entering our criteria weights:

```
cweights <- t(matrix(c(1, 0.5, 3, 2, 1, 4, 1/3, 1/4, 1),
nrow=3, ncol=3))
colnames(cweights) = c("Analytical Skills", "People
Skills", "Experience")
rownames(cweights) = c("Analytical Skills", "People
Skills", "Experience")
```

The matrix function takes values column by column so we have used the t (transpose) function to allow us to enter the weights by rows (i.e., reading left to right rather than top to bottom). We can enter our criteria weights in the same way:

```
Analytical<- t(matrix(c(1, 0.25, 4, 1/6, 4, 1, 4,
0.25, 0.25, 0.25, 1, 0.2, 6, 4, 5, 1), nrow=4,
ncol=4))
colnames(Analytical) = c("Bob", "Julie", "Pete",
"Steve")
rownames(Analytical) = c("Bob", "Julie", "Pete",
"Steve")
People <- t(matrix(c(1, 2, 5, 1, 0.5, 1, 3, 2, 0.2,
1/3, 1, 0.25, 1, 0.5, 4, 1), nrow=4,ncol=4))
colnames(People) = c("Bob", "Julie", "Pete", "Steve")
rownames(People) = c("Bob", "Julie", "Pete", "Steve")
Experience <- t(matrix(c(1, 1/3, 1/5, 1/2, 3, 1, 1/2,
2, 5, 2, 1, 3, 2, 1/2, 1/3, 1), nrow=4, ncol=4))
colnames(Experience) = c("Bob", "Julie", "Pete",
"Steve")
rownames(Experience) = c("Bob", "Julie", "Pete",
"Steve")
```

We can then make a list of the pairwise comparisons of the alternatives with respect to the criteria:

```
alternativesPairwiseComparisonsList <- list(Analytical
= Analytical, People = People, Experience =
Experience)
```

Then finally calculate the AHP result using:

```
AHP(cweights, alternativesPairwiseComparisonsList)
```

This will return the exact same AHP scores as you calculated earlier in Excel using the eigenvector method.

The MCDA package can also easily return consistency measures for pairwise matrices, for example, if you use:

```
pairwiseConsistencyMeasures(cweights)
```

```
pairwiseConsistencyMeasures(Analytical)
```

```
pairwiseConsistencyMeasures(People)
```

```
pairwiseConsistencyMeasures(Experience)
```

This will return various consistency measures for the pairwise matrices.[1] You will see that according to the CR rule that declares a matrix consistent if below 0.1, the criteria weights matrix is classed as being inconsistent. In the other three matrices, the Analytical matrix is classed as being inconsistent while the People and Experience matrices are considered consistent. Therefore, this suggests that the decision-maker should revise the criteria weights matrix and the analytical matrix. It is up to the decision maker whether he/she revises the judgements or not. Some studies show that the results obtained from inconsistent matrices are still acceptable to decision-makers in the majority of cases.[2]

4.3 Further Problems to Test Your AHP Skills

Now that you have mastered pairwise comparison methods in Excel and R why don't you try to solve the following two problems. The solutions to the problems are available on our accompanying website:http://www.smartdecisionsbook.com

---

1 We have only discussed the Consistency Ratio (CR) measure but you can read about the other measures in Siraj, S., Mikhailov, L., and Keane, J.A. (2015). Contribution of individual judgments toward inconsistency in pairwise comparisons. *European Journal of Operational Research* 242 (2) p557–567.

2 You may like to read the following academic paper for more details: Ishizaka, and Siraj. (2017). Are multi-criteria decision-making tools useful? An experimental comparative study of three methods. *European Journal of Operational Research* 246 (2) p462–471.

4.3.1 Select Equipment to Build Using AHP

An engineering company has approached you to help them decide which equipment to build. They have designed three equipment options (A, B, and C) that can be used for the same purpose but differ in terms of cost to build, reliability and accuracy. Use the pairwise comparisons below to calculate an AHP score for A, B and C.

Criteria weights:

	Cost to Build	Reliability	Accuracy
Cost to Build	1	1/2	1/4
Reliability	2	1	1/2
Accuracy	4	2	1

Pairwise comparisons for Cost to Build:

	Equipment A	Equipment B	Equipment C
Equipment A	1	1/4	1/2
Equipment B	4	1	3
Equipment C	2	1/3	1

Pairwise comparisons for Reliability:

	Equipment A	Equipment B	Equipment C
Equipment A	1	5	2
Equipment B	1/5	1	1/3
Equipment C	1/2	3	1

Pairwise comparisons for Accuracy:

	Equipment A	Equipment B	Equipment C
Equipment A	1	1/3	1/5
Equipment B	3	1	1/2
Equipment C	5	2	1

4.3.2 Select a Server to Buy Using AHP

Your company is going to purchase a new server and you have been approached to help model the decision using AHP. You are selecting from three servers (A, B and C) using four criteria: cost, power, aesthetics and reliability. Your boss has provided you with pairwise comparisons for the criteria weights and for each of the servers with respect to the three criteria:

Criteria weights:

	Cost	Power	Aesthetics	Reliability
Cost	1	3	6	1/3
Power	1/3	1	3	1/4
Aesthetics	1/6	1/3	1	1/7
Reliability	3	4	7	1

Pairwise comparisons for Cost:

	Server A	Server B	Server C
Server A	1	3	6
Server B	1/3	1	3
Server C	1/6	1/3	1

Pairwise comparisons for Power:

	Server A	Server B	Server C
Server A	1	1/2	1/5
Server B	2	1	1/3
Server C	5	3	1

Pairwise comparisons for Aesthetics:

	Server A	Server B	Server C
Server A	1	3	7
Server B	1/3	1	4
Server C	1/7	1/4	1

Pairwise comparisons for Reliability:

	Server A	Server B	Server C
Server A	1	1/2	1/3
Server B	2	1	1/2
Server C	3	2	1

5

Ideal Point Methods

One of my friends always talks about wanting to purchase his dream car when he retires. He says he wants it to look like an American muscle car, have the reliability of a Korean car, be as well engineered as a German car, be as fuel efficient as a Japanese hatchback, and drive like a French car. When I asked him to see a picture of this car he looked at me like I was an idiot and explained that it doesn't really exist. He just created an ideal hypothetical car based on the options available to him. Little did he know, he can use this ideal hypothetical car to find the best car to buy which does actually exist. This is what we will discuss in this chapter, the ideal point methods.

Ideal point methods are compensatory approaches to assess alternatives on the basis of their similarity or separation from an ideal point. The ideal point can be imagined as the best possible (or the worst possible) solution in a given scenario. The two most prominent ideal point methods are TOPSIS (Technique for Order Preference by Similarity to Ideal Solutions) and VIKOR (the acronym in Serbian translates to "Multi-criteria Optimisation and Compromise Solution"). Both methods were developed independently but are similar. The main differences between the methods are the normalisation procedures and aggregating functions. This chapter will focus on the TOPSIS method but there is an Excel example of the VIKOR method available on the book's accompanying website.

TOPSIS has been around since the 1980s[1] and has mostly been used for addressing decisions related to supply chain management, logistics, design, engineering and manufacturing.[2] The idea behind TOPSIS is that the best alternative should have the shortest distance from the best possible solution and the furthest distance from the worst possible solution (experts call

---

1 TOPSIS was first proposed by Hwang, C.L., and Yoon, K. (1981). *Multiple Attribute Decision Making: Methods and Applications*. New York: Springer-Verlag.

2 According to Behzadian, M., Otaghsara, S.K., Yazdani, M., and Ignatius, J. (2012). A state-of-the-art survey of TOPSIS applications. Expert Systems with Applications 39 (17): 13051-13069.

Smart Decisions: A Structured Approach to Decision Analysis Using MCDA, First Edition.
Edited by Richard Edgar Hodgett, Sajid Siraj, and Ellen Louise Hogg.
© 2024 John Wiley & Sons Ltd. Published 2024 by John Wiley & Sons Ltd.

these positive and negative ideal solutions). The best and worst possible solutions are hypothetical alternatives which are constructed by the decision-maker. The best scores for each criterion are selected and combined to generate this hypothetical "ideal" point and the worst scores for each criterion are combined to generate the "negative-ideal" point. TOPSIS calculates scores for each alternative by comparing Euclidean distances between the actual alternatives and the hypothesised ones. Euclidean distance is just a fancy name for the distance measured in a straight line between two points (i.e. how a bird would fly). Although Euclidean distances are most commonly considered with TOPSIS in practice, there exist other distance measures as well, for example, Manhattan distance and Chebyshev distance. Manhattan distance is measured by drawing a mix of horizontal and vertical lines between two points (e.g., how a car would travel around Manhattan) and Chebyshev distance is measured by choosing the longest line on either horizontal or vertical axis (e.g., the number of moves a King will take on a chess board). The three types of distance measures are illustrated in Figure 5.1 in a two-dimensional space.

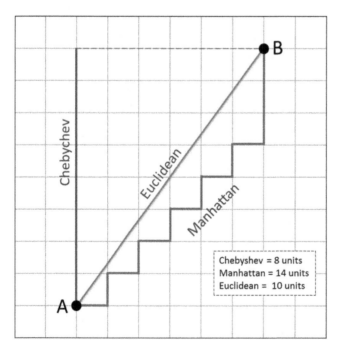

Figure 5.1 Chebyshev, Euclidean and Manhattan distance measures.

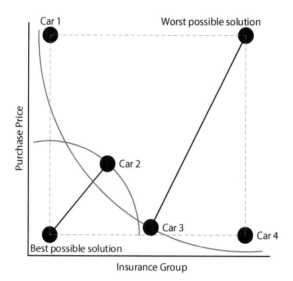

Figure 5.2 Example of how distances are used in TOPSIS.

In an n-dimensional world, these distances can be calculated using the following equations:

$$d_{\text{Chebyshev}} = \max_i |a_i - b_i|$$

$$d_{\text{Manhattan}} = \sum_{i-1}^{n} |a_i - b_i|$$

$$d_{\text{Euclidean}} = \sqrt{\sum_{i=1}^{n} (a_i - b_i)^2}$$

To illustrate how TOPSIS works, consider you want to buy a car and you have identified two criteria which you want to minimise (i.e. find the lowest value of); purchase price and insurance group. You have also shortlisted four car models which you are interested in as illustrated in Figure 5.2.

You will notice that the best possible solution is close to the origin (0,0) as you want the lowest purchase price and insurance group while the worst possible solution is far away from the origin, indicating a high purchase price and insurance group. Car 2 is the closest alternative to the positive ideal solution and Car 3 is the furthest alternative from the negative ideal solution. You will see in the example below how TOPSIS uses these measures to calculate scores for each alternative.

5.1 Select a Car to Purchase Using TOPSIS in Excel

Stephen (Richard's father) wanted to purchase a new car and after test driving nearly every make and model of car in existence he finally shortlisted three cars that he really liked. We have been told by our publisher that we can't name the real names of the cars therefore we will refer to the three cars as Fred, Betsey and Penelope (which according to a popular UK car breakdown service are some of the most popular car names given by owners!). Fred is a French hybrid that really CAPTUREs your attention, Betsey is a Romanian hatchback that James May was very excited about on Top Gear many years ago and Penelope is a South Korean city car that you could say has "10 eyes". Subtle eh?

Stephen liked driving all three cars and so wanted to make a decision on which one to buy based on other criteria. He recently retired so wanted to buy a car that was low cost but also one that would continue to be low cost to run and easy to maintain for the foreseeable future. Consequently, he selected purchase price (in £ – lower the better), insurance group (lower the better), the number of years of warranty provided (higher the better) and economy (as Miles Per Gallon (MPG) – higher the better) on which to make his car selection decision. He also selected weights for each criterion, giving the most importance to the purchase price and least importance to the economy (let's hope the price of fuel doesn't go up!). The criteria, weights, alternatives and values can be seen in the decision table shown in Table 5.1.

To start modelling this problem in Excel, enter the car selection decision matrix into Excel as shown in Figure 5.3.

Table 5.1 Decision table for the car selection problem

	Purchase Price (£)	Insurance Group	Warranty (years)	Economy (MPG)
Weight:	0.35	0.25	0.25	0.15
Fred	16,275	11	4	78.5
Betsey	11,095	11	5	74.3
Penelope	12,340	5	5	57

Figure 5.3 Decision table in Excel. (Used with permission of Microsoft).

The first step in TOPSIS is to calculate a normalised decision table using the following equation:

$$r_{ij} = \frac{x_{ij}}{\sqrt{\sum_i x_{ij}^2}}$$

This is really simple to do in Excel, simply enter in the following formula into cell C8: **=SQRT(SUMSQ(C4:C6))**

This adds the squared values of C4:C6 and finds the square root of the total. You can drag the bottom right of this cell to the right by three places to calculate $\sqrt{\sum_i x_{ij}^2}$ for all of the criteria as shown in Figure 5.4.

Next, we need to normalise all of the values in the decision matrix by dividing them by:

$$\sqrt{\sum_i x_{ij}^2}$$

To do this, insert the following formula in cell C10: **=C4/C$8**

You can drag the bottom right of this cell down two places and across by three places to calculate the normalised decision matrix (I have also centred the values and added a grey background colour) as shown in Figure 5.5.

	A	B	C	D	E	F
1						
2			Purchase Price (£)	Insurance Group	Warranty (years)	Economy (MPG)
3		Weight:	0.35	0.25	0.25	0.15
4		Fred	16,275	11	4	78.5
5		Betsey	11,095	11	5	74.3
6		Penelope	12,340	5	5	57
7						
8			23243.28398	16.34013464	8.124038405	122.1954991
9						

Figure 5.4 Decision table for calculating the normalised decision matrix. (Used with permission of Microsoft).

	A	B	C	D	E	F
1						
2			Purchase Price (£)	Insurance Group	Warranty (years)	Economy (MPG)
3		Weight:	0.35	0.25	0.25	0.15
4		Fred	16,275	11	4	78.5
5		Betsey	11,095	11	5	74.3
6		Penelope	12,340	5	5	57
7						
8			23243.28398	16.34013464	8.124038405	122.1954991
9						
10		Normalised DM:	0.700202261	0.673189067	0.492365964	0.642413187
11			0.477342187	0.673189067	0.615457455	0.608042035
12			0.530906046	0.305995031	0.615457455	0.466465626
13						

Figure 5.5 Normalised decision matrix. (Used with permission of Microsoft).

	A	B	C	D	E	F
1						
2			Purchase Price (£)	Insurance Group	Warranty (years)	Economy (MPG)
3		Weight:	0.35	0.25	0.25	0.15
4		Fred	16,275	11	4	78.5
5		Betsey	11,095	11	5	74.3
6		Penelope	12,340	5	5	57
7						
8			23243.28398	16.34013464	8.124038405	122.1954991
9						
10		Normalised DM:	0.700202261	0.673189067	0.492365964	0.642413187
11			0.477342187	0.673189067	0.615457455	0.608042035
12			0.530906046	0.305995031	0.615457455	0.466465626
13						
14		Weighted normalised DM:	0.245070791	0.168297267	0.123091491	0.096361978
15			0.167069765	0.168297267	0.153864364	0.091206305
16			0.185817116	0.076498758	0.153864364	0.069969844
17						

Figure 5.6 Weighted normalised decision matrix. (Used with permission of Microsoft).

Next, we need to multiply the values in the normalised decision matrix by their respective weights to create a weighted normalised decision matrix. To do this, insert the following formula in cell C14: **=C10*C$3**

This multiplies the value in cell C10 by its respective weight in cell C3. As the position of the weight cell (C3) has been made constant (using $), you can drag the bottom right of cell C14 down two places and across by three places to calculate the weighted normalised decision matrix as shown in Figure 5.6.

It's all been pretty easy so far, right? Well let's put one of Excel's advanced features to good use. We need to identify the best and worst possible solutions from the weighted normalised decision matrix. This is really easy to do, for example, if you consider Purchase Price where the lowest value is the best, the best possible solution would be 0.167 (i.e. the value for Betsey) and worst possible solution would be 0.245 (i.e. the value for Fred). However, instead of you manually identifying these values, let's let Excel to do the hard work. This will also allow you to conduct a sensitivity analysis later without having to manually identify the best and worst solutions.

First let's visualise the best and worst solutions using conditional formatting. We can automatically colour cells and format text based on the best and worst values. We need to do this separately for each criterion. Starting with Purchase Price, select cells C14:C16 and click on the conditional formatting button on the home tab and select New Rule as shown in Figure 5.7.

Select the Rule Type "Format only top or bottom ranked values". Then set the Bottom 1 ranked value to be filled green with a white bold font as shown in Figure 5.8.

Click OK then add a second rule for the top ranked value to be filled red with a white bold font as shown in Figure 5.9.

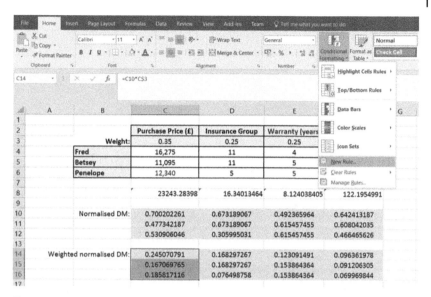

Figure 5.7 Add a new conditional formatting rule. (Used with permission of Microsoft).

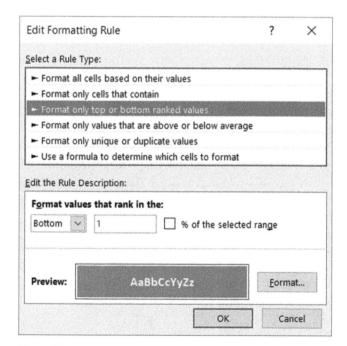

Figure 5.8 Add the formatting rule. (Used with permission of Microsoft).

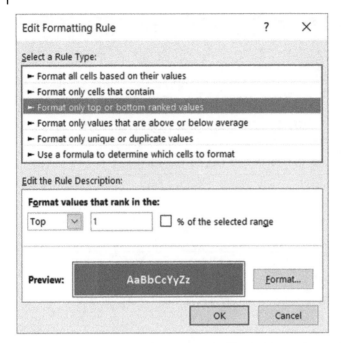

Figure 5.9 Add the second formatting rule. (Used with permission of Microsoft).

14	Weighted normalised DM:	0.245070791	0.168297267	0.123091491	0.096361978
15		0.167069765	0.168297267	0.153864364	0.091206305
16		0.185817116	0.076498758	0.153864364	0.069969844

Figure 5.10 Weighted normalised matrix with conditional formatting for purchase price. (Used with permission of Microsoft).

This will highlight the best and worst possible solutions for purchase price in green and red respectively as shown in Figure 5.10 (although as we have tried to keep the cost of the printed book to a minimum these will be in grey).

Now highlight cells E14:E16 (for warranty) and add the two conditional formatting rules shown in Figure 5.11.

As this is a maximising criterion, you set the top value as green and the bottom value as red. You will notice that two of the cells will be coloured green, this is because these cells share the same (best solution) value.

Repeat this conditional formatting proceedure for the values relating to insurance group (lower the better) and economy (higher the better). This will give you the following the image shown in Figure 5.12.

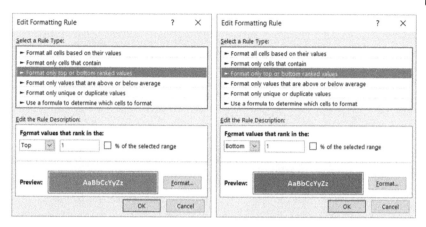

Figure 5.11 Conditional formatting rules for warranty (cells E14:16). (Used with permission of Microsoft).

14	Weighted normalised DM:	0.245070791	0.168297267	0.123091491	0.096361978
15		0.167069765	0.168297267	0.153864364	0.091206305
16		0.185817116	0.076498758	0.153864364	0.069969844

Figure 5.12 Weighted normalised matrix with conditional formatting. (Used with permission of Microsoft).

Now that you can visually see the best and worst possible solutions, we need to be able to identify them in Excel formula for calculating their separation from each alternative. We can do this using the SMALL and LARGE functions in Excel, where LARGE identifies the largest values and SMALL identifies the smallest values. As we want to find the first largest and first smallest values we use LARGE(data, 1) and SMALL(data, 1) respectively.

To calculate the separation matrix between each alternative and the best possible alternative enter the following formulas into the respective cells:

C18: =(C14-SMALL(C$14:C$16,1))^2
D18: =(D14-SMALL(D$14:D$16,1))^2
E18: =(E14-LARGE(E$14:E$16,1))^2
F18: =(F14-LARGE(F$14:F$16,1))^2

As the best possible solution cells are constant, you can drag the bottom right of these cells down by two places to create the separation matrix as shown in Figure 5.13.

To calculate the final separation values for each alternative, insert the following formula in cell G18:

=SQRT(SUM(C18:F18))

17						
18	Separation from best possible:	0.00608416	0.008426966	0.00094697	0	
19		0	0.008426966	0	2.6581E-05	
20		0.000351463	0	0	0.000696545	
21						

Figure 5.13 Separation matrix from the best possible solution. (Used with permission of Microsoft).

18	Separation from best possible:	0.00608416	0.008426966	0.00094697	0	0.12433
19		0	0.008426966	0	2.6581E-05	0.09194
20		0.000351463	0	0	0.000696545	0.03237

Figure 5.14 Separation from the best possible solution. (Used with permission of Microsoft).

You can then drag the bottom right of this cell down by two places to give the separation of each alternative from the positive ideal solution as shown in Figure 5.14.

To calculate the separation for each alternative from the negative ideal solutions enter in the following formula into the respective cells:

C22: =(C14-LARGE(C$14:C$16,1))^2
D22: =(D14-LARGE(D$14:D$16,1))^2
E22: =(E14-SMALL(E$14:E$16,1))^2
F22: =(F14-SMALL(F$14:F$16,1))^2

Similarly to earlier, you can drag the bottom right of these cells down by two places to show the separation matrix. Then to calculate the separation for each alternative, insert the following formula in cell G22:

=SQRT(SUM(C22:F22))

After dragging the bottom right of cell G22 down by two cells you will have the Euclidean distance for the separation between each alternative and the best/worst possible solutions as shown in Figure 5.15.

18	Separation from best possible:	0.00608416	0.008426966	0.00094697	0	0.12433
19		0	0.008426966	0	2.6581E-05	0.09194
20		0.000351463	0	0	0.000696545	0.03237
21						
22	Separation from worst possible:	0	0	0	0.000696545	0.02639
23		0.00608416	0	0.00094697	0.000450987	0.0865
24		0.003510998	0.008426966	0.00094697	0	0.11351

Figure 5.15 Separations from the best and worst possible solutions. (Used with permission of Microsoft).

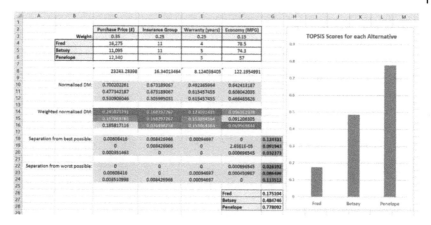

Figure 5.16   TOPSIS results with bar chart. (Used with permission of Microsoft).

Now we can use these values to calculate the TOPSIS scores for each alternative by dividing the separation from the worst possible solution by the sum of the best and worst possible solutions. In cell G26 input the following formula:

=G22/(G18+G22)

You can drag the bottom right of this cell down by two places to get the scores for each alternative. You can then select the data and insert a bar chart to visualise the results as shown in Figure 5.16.

As you can see the TOPSIS analysis scored Penelope as the best option followed by Betsey. Fred received the lowest TOPSIS score. After seeing the results, Stephen requested that the the robustness of the results be checked through a sensitivity analysis to see if certain scenarios give the same recommendation. Try the following scenarios (remember to revert the changes after testing each scenario):

- Stephen decided that the criteria weights should be equal, see if the results change if each criterion is given a weight of 0.25.
- The manufacturer of Penelope reduced the warranty to 3 years.
- Due to a special promotion the price of Betsey has been reduced by £2,000.
- Penelope's insurance group classification changed to 8.

As you can see Penelope is a very strong alternative and given this Stephen made his decision and ordered a Penelope (as shown in Figure 5.17):

Figure 5.17 Stephen made his decision and ordered a Penelope.

5.2 Select a Car to Purchase Using TOPSIS in R

A function for TOPSIS is available in the MCDA package for R. To install the MCDA package use `install.packages("MCDA")` then use `library("MCDA")` to add this package to your R library.

Next, we need to input the decision matrix, we can do this with:

```
DM <- matrix(c(16275, 11, 4, 78.5, 11095, 11, 5, 74.3,
12340, 5, 5, 57), nrow=3, ncol=4, byrow=TRUE)
```

Then, if you wish, you can add the criterion and alternative names to the matrix using:

```
colnames(DM) <- c("Purchase Price", "Insurance Group",
"Warranty", "Economy")

row.names(DM) <- c("Fred", "Betsey", "Penelope")
```

Now when you call back DM you will see the full decision matrix with the names of the alternatives and criteria present. Next, we need to input the weights and whether each criterion is minimising or maximising, this can be done with the following:

```
weights <- c(0.35, 0.25, 0.25, 0.15)

criteriaMinMax <- c("min", "min", "max", "max")
```

You can, if you wish, also add the criteria names to weights and criteriaMin-Max with the following:

```
names(weights) <- colnames(DM)
```

```
names(criteriaMinMax) <- colnames(DM)
```

Now we can use the TOPSIS function in the MCDA package to calculate the results with:

```
TOPSIS(DM, weights, criteriaMinMax)
```

As you will see, the results are identical the results identified in the Excel analysis.

5.3 Further Problems to Test Your TOPSIS Skills

Now that you have mastered ideal point methods in Excel and R why don't you try to solve the following two problems. The solutions to the problems are available on our accompanying website:

http://www.smartdecisionsbook.com

5.3.1 Select Office Space Using TOPSIS

	Weight	Property 1	Property 2	Property 3
Property Price ($) • minimising	0.4	220,000	350,000	185,000
Distance from current offices (m) • minimising	0.3	200	50	450
Attractiveness (/10) • maximising	0.15	7	9	4
Facilities (/10) • maximising	0.15	9	7	9

Your company is going to purchase a new property to use as office space. You want the property to be low cost, close to your current offices, look attractive and have good bathroom/kitchen facilities. You have identified three properties that meet your criteria but you are finding it difficult to select the best property from the data below:

Using this data and the TOPSIS technique, provide a recommendation and explanation for what property your company should purchase.

5.3.2   Select Venue for Lunch Using TOPSIS

You have recently been promoted and being the nice person that you are, you decide to take your colleagues out to lunch to celebrate. There are four cafés near to your office that serve lunch. Having been to them many times before you have created the following table:

	Weight	Café North	Café South	Café East	Café West
Lunch set menu price ($) • Minimising	0.3	20	16	35	20
Location (km) • Minimising	0.2	2.1	3	0.2	1.8
Atmosphere (/10) • Maximising	0.2	8	4	10	6
Range of products (/10) • Maximising	0.1	8	7	5	8
Food quality (/10) • Maximising	0.2	7	6	9	7

Using this data and the TOPSIS technique, provide a recommendation and explanation for which café you should take your colleagues to.

6

Outranking Methods

Outranking methods are relatively complicated techniques which offer a number of distinct advantages over other decision analysis methods. We find the easiest way to explain these advantages is through an example. Consider a family which has recently moved to a new home and are trying to identify the most appropriate school for their child. In order to assess their options, they compare a handful of schools nearby. They find that there is no clear winner with respect to all the criteria that the family considers important.

School A is much closer to home than School B but the latest school evaluation reports rank School A very low, so mum has vetoed against it. They have also identified a third school, School C which is ranked higher than the other two schools but it is further away from home. Although School C is further away from the family home than School B, Dad is indifferent between the two schools in terms of distances as it only takes him a few more minutes to drive to School C in comparison to School B with traffic. The fourth and final option, School D is half the distance of travelling to School B and was ranked as average in the latest school evaluation reports. Although School D is ranked lower than Schools B and C, mum does not veto it as it isn't as bad as School A, and dad prefers this school over School B on the distance criterion. Which one should the family select?

This represents a common decision-making problem in practice as we often confront situations where someone vetoes against some of the alternatives. Also, some people may find minor differences to be insignificant in their decision-making exercise. In such situations, the aggregation approaches we discussed earlier generally fail to handle these requirements, and therefore become unsuitable. Unlike the aggregation-based methods, outranking methods can still be used in these complicated situations involving insignificance and vetoing. This chapter will introduce one of the most prominent outranking methods called ELECTRE which was proposed by a French Professor named Bernard Roy,[1] who is one of the most famous names in the field of decision-making.

---

1 First discussed in French by Roy, B. (1968). Classement et choix en présence de points de vue multiples (la méthode ELECTRE). *La Revue d'Informatique et de Recherche Opérationelle (RIRO)* volume 2 (8): 57–75.

Smart Decisions: A Structured Approach to Decision Analysis Using MCDA, First Edition.
Edited by Richard Edgar Hodgett, Sajid Siraj, and Ellen Louise Hogg.
© 2024 John Wiley & Sons Ltd. Published 2024 by John Wiley & Sons Ltd.

6.1   Introduction to ELECTRE

The ELECTRE method is based on three fundamental relations between alternatives: indifference, preference, and veto. The term indifference represents a situation where the difference between two choices is so small that the decision-maker considers it unimportant. Recall the school example above, the distances for Schools B and C were considered indifferent as the difference in travel time was only a few minutes. Let's formulate indifference as the following rule:

> Option 1 is **INDIFFERENT** to Option 2 when the **difference between** their scores remains **below an indifference threshold**

On the other hand, if the difference between two options become large enough, the decision-maker can clearly state one option is preferred over the other one. In our school example, the dad clearly preferred School D over Schools B and C with respect to their distances from home. Let's formulate difference as the following rule:

> Option 1 is **STRICTLY PREFERRED** over Option 2 when **the score for Option 1 minus the score for Option 2 exceeds a threshold for preference**

There can also be a situation where the difference between two options is so large that the decision-maker removes the inferior option from any further consideration. In other words, the weaker option can be vetoed in favour of the much stronger option. Let's formulate this as the following rule:

> Option2 is **REJECTED (VETOED)** when **the score for Option 1 minus the score for Option 2 exceeds a threshold for veto**

Between the three different thresholds you can assume different levels of preference. For example, between the indifference and preference thresholds you can assume weak preference and between the preference and veto threshold you can assume strong preference as shown in Figure 6.1.

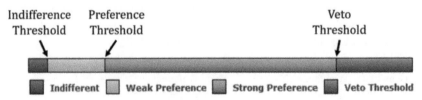

Figure 6.1   Visualisation of ELECTRE thresholds.

To better understand ELECTRE thresholds, let us assume the performance table for the four schools as shown in Table 6.1:

Table 6.1 Performance table for schools.

	School A	School B	School C	School D
Location	0.2 miles	2.3 miles	2.4 miles	1 mile
Quality	3/10	9/10	10/10	7/10

Note that this example is kept simple with only two criteria (of location and quality) but in real life there will likely be many more criteria to consider. A visual representation of the problem is shown in Figure 6.2.

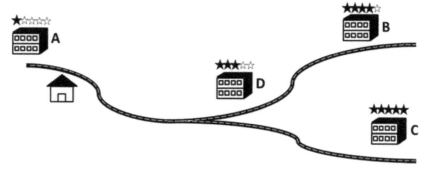

Figure 6.2 Visual representation of the four schools example.

Let's compare the distances first. The distances of B and C from home are 2.3 and 2.4 miles respectively. The dad considered this difference negligible so we can inquire with him about this more, for example, would he consider the difference of 0.2 miles "negligible" or not? Or in other words, at what threshold would he stop considering the difference negligible. If the dad states the threshold of 0.2 miles then any two options having difference of less than 0.2 miles should be considered indifferent, or in other words, one should not be preferred over another under the distance criterion. The family could have suggested the following thresholds of indifference:

Indifference for	q_i
Distance	0.2 mile
Quality	1 point on scale

This indifference relation can be represented in mathematical form as below:

$$aI_ib: |g_i(a) - g_i(b)| < q_i$$

Here, a and b are the two options compared, I_i represents the indifference relationship under the criterion i. The $g_i(a)$ and $g_i(b)$ are the performance scores of a and b under the criterion i, respectively. The straight lines around these performance scores imply the absolute value of their difference, and finally, q_i is the indifference threshold.

This may look like mathematical gobbledygook for someone who is not familiar with mathematical notations but this equation is nothing more than what we discussed earlier about the indifference relationship.

In the school example, dad could suggest that anything more than the difference of 1 mile with regards to distance would definitely be preferred over another option while mum could suggest that an improvement of 2 points on the quality scale would be a clear improvement. Therefore, the following table can be constructed for thresholds of preference:

Preference threshold for	p_i
Distance	1 mile
Quality	2 points on scale

This preference relation can also be formulated mathematically as:

$$aP_ib: g_i(a) - g_i(b) > p_i$$

Here the performance score for a is larger than that for b to an extent that the difference exceeds p_i which is the threshold for strict preference.

6.1.1 Concordance and Discordance

Based on these relationships we can establish an assertion about whether option a is at least as good as option b. This assertion holds if $g(a) - g(b)$ remains above $-q$ while this assertion clearly does not hold if $g(a) - g(b)$ remains less than $-p$. This can be formulated as a concordance measure for a single criterion i as below:

$$c_i(a,b) = \begin{cases} 1 & g_i(a) \geq g_i(b) - q_i \\ 0 & g_i(a) \leq g_i(b) - p \\ \dfrac{\left|p_i - (g_i(b) - g_i(a))\right|}{p_i - q_i} & \textit{otherwise} \end{cases}$$

The concordance values can be calculated for our school example as below:

$c_{DISTANCE}$	A	B	C	D		$c_{QUALITY}$	A	B	C	D
A	1	1	1	1		A	1	0	0	0
B	0	1	1	0		B	1	1	1	1
C	0	1	1	0		C	1	1	1	1
D	0.25	1	1	1		D	1	0	0	1

Note that the concordance values for distance criterion are reversed due to the fact that distance is a cost criterion, which means, the higher the distance from school, the lower the performance.

We can calculate an overall measure, termed as concordance, by taking the weighted average of all the individual strengths of these criteria, i.e.,

$$C(a,b) = \frac{\sum_i w_i c_i(a,b)}{\sum_i w_i}$$

Where w_i is the weight assigned to criterion i.

Considering the school example, the family may decide that the quality of school is three times more important than its distance from home, and therefore we can obtain the overall concordance as below, using the weights of 0.25 and 0.75 for distance and quality respectively:

	A	B	C	D
A	1	0.25	0.25	0.25
B	0.75	1	1	0.75
C	0.75	1	1	0.75
D	0.8125	0.25	0.25	1

So far, we have explained the indifference and preference relations with the help of distance criterion in our school example. Let's turn to the quality criterion for a moment and recall that mum vetoed against School A due to its low ranking. Mum seems to have a veto threshold of around 4 points. Although there is no veto on the distance criterion, we can assume that dad considers 3.5 miles to be too high a distance to travel, and therefore, the following table can be constructed for veto thresholds:

Veto threshold	v_i
Distance	3.5 miles
Quality	4 points on scale

The veto relation can be formulated mathematically as:

$$aV_ib: g_i(a) - g_i(b) < -v_i$$

Where V_i is used to describe the relationship that option a has been forbidden due to very large difference (i.e., v_i) from b.

Based on this relationship, we can describe the discordance value as below:

$$d_i(a,b) = \begin{cases} 0 & g_i(a) \geq g_i(b) - p_i \\ 1 & g_i(a) \leq g_i(b) - v_i \\ \dfrac{(g_i(b) - g_i(a)) - p_i}{v_i - p_i} & \text{otherwise} \end{cases}$$

Note that the two equations for concordance and discordance consist of three parts. This can be better visualised in Figure 6.3 where these three parts are shown in the form of three connected lines (see concordance in the upper figure and discordance in the lower figure).

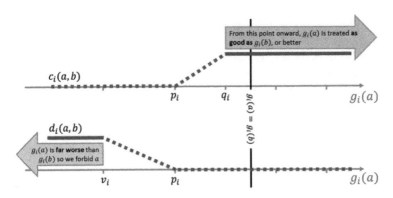

Figure 6.3 Visual illustration of concordance and discordance.

The discordance values can be calculated for our school example as below:

$d_{DISTANCE}$	A	B	C	D	$d_{QUALITY}$	A	B	C	D
A	0	0	0	0	A	0	1	1	1
B	0.44	0	0	0.12	B	0	0	0	0
C	0.48	0	0	0.16	C	0	0	0	0
D	0	0	0	0	D	0	0	0.5	0

6.1.2 Credibility

Let's put it all together now. Consider a proposition that option a is at least as good as option b. If this proposition holds then ideally we expect all the discordance values to be 0, and the credibility of this proposition can therefore be measured by overall concordance, i.e.,

$$S(a,b) = C(a,b)$$

This is true in situations where discordance values are zero, however, we add some level of flexibility in order to incorporate the non-ideal situations, i.e., we expect the concordance value to be higher than the discordance value. If this condition is violated, i.e., at least one discordance value turns out to be higher than the overall concordance, then the credibility is obtained in the following way:

$$S(a,b) = C(a,b) \prod_{d_i(a,b) > C(a,b)} \frac{1 - d_i(a,b)}{1 - C(a,b)}$$

Note that the product symbol is only applicable to the situations where $d_i(a,b) > C(a,b)$. Due to this fact, the numerator value inside the product expression is always smaller than the denominator value. In other words, these ratio values always remain between 0 and 1, and hence the credibility value gets reduced by a fraction whenever we have more discordance than concordance. The credibility value of 0 implies that this option is forbidden; and this occurs when at least one of the discordance values is equal to 1.

In our school example, the discordance value for School A against School B became so high for the quality criterion that School A lost its credibility, and therefore, mum vetoed against School A.

This credibility value can be calculated for any pair of options in hand and, therefore, we can construct a table or matrix for all these pairwise comparisons. The following credibility table can be constructed for our school example:

	A	B	C	D
A	1	0	0	0
B	0.75	1	1	0.75
C	0.75	1	1	0.75
D	0.8125	0.25	0.166667	1

The first row of the credibility table clearly shows that School A has no credibility over all the other three options (i.e., $S(a,:) = 0$).

6.1.3 Distillation

Looking at the credibility table, we can see that Schools B and C have the highest credibility values out of all the calculated ones (see the values for B and C with 1). We can use this highest value as a standard to describe the outranking relation. For example, the value of $S(D,B)$ is equal to 0.25 which is very much smaller than 1 (which is the highest value), therefore we suggest that this value of 0.25 be removed and only focus on strong outranking relations.

We can set a threshold value to decide which of these relations are strong enough to be kept for distillation process (to be discussed shortly). A common threshold value used in practice is 0.3 so based on this value we can eliminate all the credibility values less than 0.7 (i.e., 1 – 0.3) which will end up in the following table:

	A	B	C	D
A	–			
B	1	–	1	1
C	1	1	–	1
D	1			–

This table can be used to describe the outranking relationship, i.e., option 1 outranks option 2 if option 1 is as good as option 2 but option 2 is not as good as option 1. The indifference relationship holds when each of the two options is as good as the other one. In our school example, the three Schools B, C, and D clearly outrank School A as they are all as good as School A but School A is not as good as the three schools. Similarly, the two schools, B and C outrank school D using the same principle. School B and School C have an indifferent relationship because School B is as good as School C while School C is also as good as School B.

Based on this information, we can sort our options in a descending or ascending order. For each option, calculate its column sum from its row sum, that is, the difference between the number of instances where it outranked others and the number of instances where it was outranked by others. We select the option with highest score as the top ranked option (Rank 1). For further processing of the remaining options, we simply remove this top ranked option from the table (deleting its respective row and column) and then perform the same calculations of (row sum – column sum) again. We keep repeating this process until all the options are assigned a rank.

Let's do this for the school example, our first step is to calculate the row sum and column sum for each school, i.e.,

	Row sum	Column sum	Score
A	0	3	−3
B	3	1	2
C	3	1	2
D	1	2	−1

The schools B and C turn have the highest score in the first iteration so we can assign both B and C to be the top-ranked options. For second ranking, we remove the two rows related to B and C, and obtain the following scores:

	Row sum	Column sum	Score
A	0	1	−1
D	1	0	1

The second step suggests D as the next best option (Figure 6.4), so therefore, we end up in the following descending order:

Figure 6.4 Descending distillation.

We can also perform the ascending distillation in the same way by distilling the lowest score instead of the highest one in each iteration.

6.2   ELECTRE in Microsoft Excel

Now that we know each step in the process of decision making for ELECTRE, let's roll up our sleeves and implement it in Microsoft Excel. We will use the same school example so that we can easily refer to the calculations and results mentioned earlier. First of all, enter the performance scores for all four schools with respect to location and quality, as shown in Figure 6.5. Along with these

	A	B	C	D	E	F	G	H	I	J	K	L
1												
2		Inputs										
3			School A	School B	School C	School D		q	p	v	w	
4		Location	0.2	2.3	2.4	1		0.2	1	3.5	0.25	
5		Quality	3	9	10	7		1	2	4	0.75	
6												

Figure 6.5   Schools performance and threshold data entered in Excel.

performance scores, we need the three thresholds of indifference, preference, and veto along with the weight of importance for each criterion. All these values are shown in Figure 6.5 on the right side of the performance table.

The first step in our calculation is to calculate concordance and discordance. Recall the concordance equation visualised in Figure 6.1 as three connected lines, we can use the nested IF statements to implement the whole equation in a single step but this will become too complicated so let's first calculate the linear equation for concordance and then we can clip these values between 0 (the lower bound) and 1 (the upper bound) if required. The linear equation to calculate concordance is shown in Figure 6.6 where arrows highlight which cells are involved in this calculation. We show these calculations for only one cell (i.e., C12) but, as one would expect, these calculations can be repeated for all the cells in the concordance tables (for both location and quality).

	B	School A	School B	School C	School D		q	p	v	w
2	Inputs									
4	Location	0.2	2.3	2.4	1		0.2	1	3.5	0.25
5	Quality	3	9	10	7		1	2	4	0.75

			Location					Quality		
8	Concordance									
10	Linear equation for concordance									
11		1.25	3.875	4	2.25		2	-4	-5	-2
12		=($I$4-($D$4-C$4))/($I$4-$H$4)					8	2	1	4
13		-1.5	1.125	1.25	-0.5		9	3	2	5
14		0.25	2.875	3	1.25		6	0	-1	2

Figure 6.6 Linear equation to calculate partial concordance.

Now that we have the raw values for partial concordance, we need all the values above one to be clipped to one, which is the upper bound, and similarly, all the values below zero to be clipped to zero, the lower bound. Figure 6.7 shows how to clip the values with the help of IF statements in MS Excel. The first IF tests for the upper bound clips the value to 1 if the test succeeds, otherwise the second IF is activated to test for the lower bound in which case the value is clipped to 0 if it turns out to be less than 0.

	B	C	D	E	F	G	H	I	J	K
10	Linear equation for concordance									
11		1.25	3.875	4	2.25		2	-4	-5	-2
12		-1.375	1.25	1.375	-0.375		8	2	1	4
13		1.5	1.125	1.25	-0.5		9	3	2	5
14		0.25	2.875	3	1.25		6	0	-1	2
15	Partial concordance									
16		1	1	1	1		1	0	0	0
17		=IF(C12>1, 1, IF(C12<0, 0, C12))			0		1	1	1	1
18		0	1	1	0		1	1	1	1
19		0.25	1	1	1		1	0	0	1

Figure 6.7 Calculating partial concordance bounded between 0 and 1.

The overall concordance value can simply be calculated using the weighted sum of the values calculated for each criterion. As shown in Figure 6.8, the concordance for School B over School A is calculated in cell C23 from the sum of two values obtained by multiplying partial concordance values in C17 and H17 with their respective weights in the cells K4 and K5.

	B	C	D	E	F	G	H	I	J	K	L
2	Inputs										
3		School A	School B	School C	School D		q	p	v	w	
4	Location	0.2	2.3	2.4	1		0.2	1	3.5	0.25	
5	Quality	3	9	10	7		1	2	4	0.75	
6											
15	Partial concordance										
16		1	1	1	1		1	0	0	0	
17		0	1	1	0		1	1	1	1	
18		0	1	1	0		1	1	1	1	
19		0.25	1	1	1		1	0	0	1	
20											
21	Overall concordance										
22		1	0.25	0.25	0.25						
23		=C17*$K$4+H17*$K$5		1	0.75						
24		0.75	1	1	0.75						
25		0.8125	0.25	0.25	1						

Figure 6.8 Calculating overall concordance for each pair of schools.

The values for discordance can be calculated in a similar way to how we calculated for concordance, i.e., applying the linear equation model first and then clipping the value between 0 and 1, as shown in Figure 6.9.

	B	C	D	E	F	G	H	I	J	K	L
29			Location						Quality		
30	Linear equation for discordance										
31		-0.4	-1.24	-1.28	-0.72		-1	2	2.5	1	
32		=((SD$4-C$4)-$I$4)/($J$4-$I$4)			0.12		-4	-1	-0.5	-2	
33		0.48	-0.36	-0.4	0.16		-4.5	-1.5	-1	-2.5	
34		-0.08	-0.92	-0.96	-0.4		-3	0	0.5	-1	
35	Partial discordance										
36		0	0	0	0		0	1	1	1	
37		0.44	0	0	0.12		0	0	0	0	
38		0.48	0	0	0.16		0	0	0	0	
39		0	0	0	0		0	0	0.5	0	

Figure 6.9 Calculating partial discordance.

Now that we have obtained both concordance and discordance values, we can calculate the credibility in two steps, i.e., first we calculate the adjustment factor from each criterion if the discordance value is greater than its respective concordance value (see Figure 6.10), and then we multiply all these factors with the overall concordance in order to obtain the final credibility score (see Figure 6.11). Note that the figures demonstrate these calculations for only a single cell but we need to calculate this for each pairwise comparison of schools.

A	B	C	D	E	F	G	H	I	J	K	L
21	**Overall concordance**										
22		1	0.25	0.25	0.25						
23		0.75	1	1	0.75						
35	Partial discordance										
36		0	0	0	0		0	1	1	1	
37		0.44	0	0	0.12		0	0	0	0	
38		0.48	0	0	0.16		0	0	0	0	
42	**Credibility**										
43				Location					Quality		
44	Credibility adjustment factor										
45		1	1	1	1		1	0	0	0	
46	=IF(C37>C23, (1-C37)/(1-C23), 1)		1	1		1	1	1	1		
47		1	1	1	1		1	1	1	1	
48		1	1	1	1		1	1	0.66667	1	

Figure 6.10 Calculating credibility adjustment factor for each criterion.

A	B	C	D	E	F	G	H	I	J	K	L
21	**Overall concordance**										
22		1	0.25	0.25	0.25						
23		0.75	1	1	0.75						
42	**Credibility**										
43				Location					Quality		
44	Credibility adjustment factor										
45		1	1	1	1		1	0	0	0	
46		1	1	1	1		1	1	1	1	
47		1	1	1	1		1	1	1	1	
48		1	1	1	1		1	1	0.66667	1	
49											
50	**Final credibility**										
51			0	0	0						
52		=C23*C46*H46		1	0.75						
53		0.75	1	1	0.75						
54		0.8125	0.25	0.16667	1						

Figure 6.11 Calculating the credibility matrix.

After calculating the credibility scores, we are ready for the final phase of distillation. As discussed earlier, we choose a threshold to decide which of these credibility scores are strong enough to sustain. In other words, if the credibility score is high enough, we will set it to 1, otherwise 0. The calculations for the cell C63 (i.e., representing credibility of School B against A) is shown in Figure 6.12.

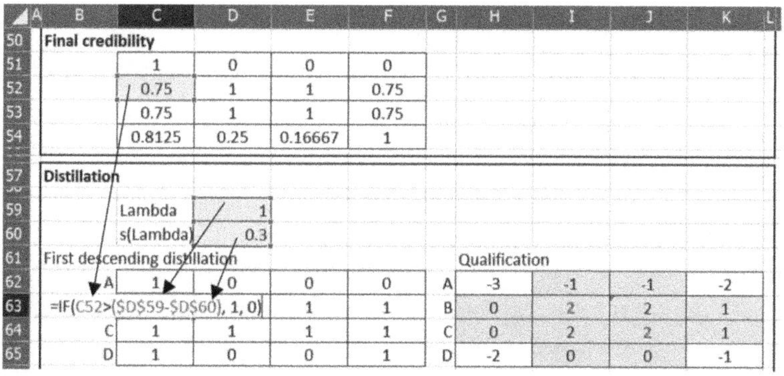

Figure 6.12 Pre-processing steps for distillation.

This Boolean table (only containing values 0 or 1) can be used to reach the overall ranking of each option. We simply calculate the sum of row minus the sum of column for each school to quantify their qualification score for the top position. In Figure 6.13, we have demonstrated this for the diagonal values (i.e., second row, second column) due to the fact that we are only interested in the diagonal values, i.e., we want to assess how many options are dominated by the given option (i.e., sum of its row) and how many options are dominating the given option (i.e., sum of its column). The difference of these two numbers will quantify the qualification level of each option. For example, based on these scores, we can conclude that Schools B and C both have jointly scored the highest, i.e., 4–2 = 2. So we declare B and C to be on first rank.

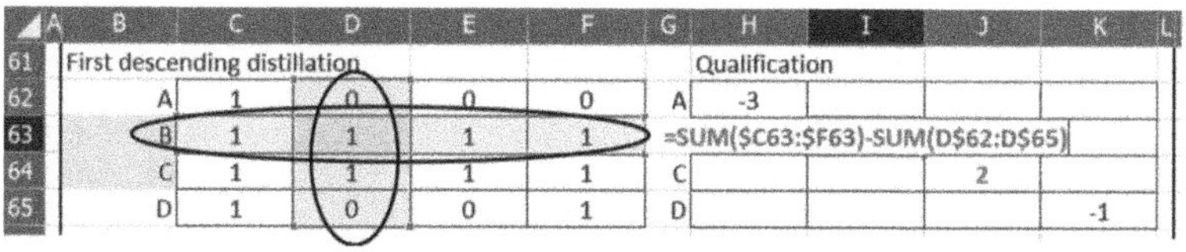

Figure 6.13 Descending distillation process – iteration 1.

Now that Schools B and C are processed, we remove their information from the distillation table and repeat the same process for the remaining items. We keep doing this until all the options are processed. As shown in Figure 6.14, the second iteration of descending distillation suggests that School D is the next most suitable option with the qualification score of 1, and this leaves School A on the lowest rank with the qualification score of –1.

◢A	B	C	D	E	F	G	H	I
66	Second descending distillation on remaining alternatives							
67	A	1	0			A	-1	0
68	D	1	1			D	0	1
69	**Descending order**							
70		B,C	D	A		A	1	

Figure 6.14 Descending distillation process – iteration 2.

The distillation process can also be used in reverse order, i.e., instead of using descending order, we can process it in an ascending order by selecting the lowest score first and then repeating the process on remaining options. Figure 6.15 shows the outcome of each iteration when the ascending distillation is used instead of the descending one. Note that we have obtained the same ranking except in reverse order but this cannot be generalized – descending distillation and ascending distillation may produce slightly different ranking schemes.

◢A	B	C	D	E	F	G	H	I	J	K	L
73	First ascending distillation						Qualification				
74	A	1	0	0	0	A	-3	-1	-1	-2	
75	B	1	1	1	1	B	0	2	2	1	
76	C	1	1	1	1	C	0	2	2	1	
77	D	1	0	0	1	D	-2	0	0	-1	
78	Second ascending distillation on remaining alternatives										
79	B	1	1	1			1	1	0		
80	C	1	1	1			1	1	0		
81	D	0	0	1			-1	-1	-2		
82	Third ascending distillation on remaining alternatives										
83	B	1	1				0	0			
84	C	1	1				0	0			
85	**Ascending order**										
86		A	D	B,C							

Figure 6.15 Ascending distillation process – iterations 1 to 3.

6.3 ELECTRE in R

Inputs									
	School A	School B	School C	School D		q	p	v	w
Location	0.2	2.3	2.4	1		0.2	1	3.5	0.25
Quality	3	9	10	7		1	2	4	0.75

First, let's install the MCDA package and add it to your library:

```
install.packages("MCDA")
library("MCDA")
```

Then we will setup the information from the school example into a decision matrix:

```
scores <- matrix( c( -0.2,-2.3,-2.4,-1,  3,9,10,7 ),
nrow = 4, dimnames = list(c("School-A","School-B",
"School-C", "School-D"), c("Location","Quality")))
```

Then set our variables for q, p, v and w:

```
q <- c( 0.2, 1)
p <- c(   1, 2)
v <- c( 3.5, 4)
w <- c(0.25, 0.75)
```

Finally, let's use the ELECTRE function in the MCDA package to calculate the results:

```
res <- ELECTRE3(scores, q, p, v, w)
```

Then return the results using:

```
print(res)
```

$concordance

```
          [,1] [,2] [,3] [,4]
[1,] 1.0000 0.25 0.25 0.25
[2,] 0.7500 1.00 1.00 0.75
[3,] 0.7500 1.00 1.00 0.75
[4,] 0.8125 0.25 0.25 1.00
```

$discordance

```
, , 1
      [,1] [,2] [,3] [,4]
[1,] 0.00    0    0 0.00
[2,] 0.44    0    0 0.12
[3,] 0.48    0    0 0.16
[4,] 0.00    0    0 0.00
, , 2
      [,1] [,2] [,3] [,4]
[1,]    0    1  1.0    1
[2,]    0    0  0.0    0
[3,]    0    0  0.0    0
[4,]    0    0  0.5    0
```

$credibility

```
          [,1] [,2]       [,3] [,4]
[1,] 1.0000 0.00 0.0000000 0.00
[2,] 0.7500 1.00 1.0000000 0.75
[3,] 0.7500 1.00 1.0000000 0.75
[4,] 0.8125 0.25 0.1666667 1.00
```

```
$dominance
       [,1] [,2] [,3] [,4]
[1,]    1    0    0    0
[2,]    1    1    1    1
[3,]    1    1    1    1
[4,]    1    0    0    1
$scoring
[1] -3  2   2  -1
```

This scoring can be translated as School A = −3, School B = 2, School C = 2 and School D = −1.

Giving us the same ranking as the Excel method in descending order B and C are equal then A then D.

6.4 Further Problems to Test Your ELECTRE Skills

Now that you have mastered ELECTRE methods in Excel and R why don't you try to solve the following two problems. The solutions to the problems are available on our accompanying website:

http://www.smartdecisionsbook.com

1) You are trying to decide where to go on your summer beach holiday. You have completed the following table of the three destinations based on the following criteria weather (average hours of sun per day), hotel (customer review rating/10) and price (£ per night). You have also assigned criteria weights (w), indifference thresholds (q) preference thresholds (p) and veto (v).

	Weather	Hotel	Price
Beach A	10	9	90
Beach B	6	8	130
Beach C	8	7	95
Beach D	7	5	100
q	1	1	8
p	1.1	2	5
v	6	3	30
w	50	20	30

What is the best holiday destination?

2) You are buying a house and want to decide between four different houses. You are judging on size (SQ meters) price (£) and distance from work (miles). You have also assigned criteria weights (w), indifference thresholds (q) preference thresholds (p) and veto (v).

	Price	Size
House A	220 000	625
House B	250 000	602
House C	150 000	800
House D	120 000	545
q	12	8
p	5	6
v	30 000	200
w	30	70

Which is the best home to purchase?

7

PROMETHEE

As discussed in the previous chapter, the ELECTRE method is based on three fundamental relations between alternatives: indifference, preference, and veto. PROMETHEE is another outranking method (originally proposed by Brans in 1982[1]) which is quite widely used and is based on similar ideas of indifference and preference; however, it does not support the idea of vetoing and therefore reduces the complexity in its model. Recalling the two ideas of indifference, we can reproduce those relations here as

$$aI_ib: \left|g_i(a) - g_i(b)\right| < q_i$$

Option1 IS INDIFFERENT TO Option2 when
The difference of their scores remains below an indifference threshold and

$$aP_ib: g_i(a) - g_i(b) > p_i$$

Option1 IS STRICTLY PREFERRED OVER Option2 when
Option1 score minus Option2 score exceeds a threshold for preference.

In the first equation, a and b are the two compared options, and I_i represents the indifference relationship under the criterion i. The $g_i(a)$ and $g_i(b)$ are the performance scores of a and b under the criterion i, respectively. In the second equation, the performance score for a is larger than that for b to an extent that the difference exceeds p_i which is the threshold for strict preference.

Unlike ELECTRE where these relations were used to calculate concordance and discordance, we calculate the preference dominance relation based on a preference function. There are six preference functions that are originally proposed as part of the PROMETHEE approach. These functions are Usual, U-shape, V-shape, Level (Stair-shape), Linear, and Gaussian. Although each of

---

1 J.P. Brans. L'ingénièrie de la décision; Elaboration d'instruments d'aide à la décision. La méthode PROMETHEE. In R. Nadeau and M. Landry, editors, L'aide à la décision: Nature, Instruments et Perspectives d'Avenir, pages 183–213, Québec, Canada, 1982. Presses de l'Université Laval.

Smart Decisions: A Structured Approach to Decision Analysis Using MCDA, First Edition.
Edited by Richard Edgar Hodgett, Sajid Siraj, and Ellen Louise Hogg.
© 2024 John Wiley & Sons Ltd. Published 2024 by John Wiley & Sons Ltd.

these functions can be described mathematically, their graphical representations would give a better idea to compare them and to evaluate which one is most suitable for your problem. These shapes have been visualised in Figure 7.1.

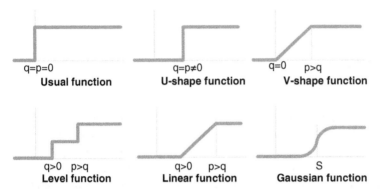

Figure 7.1 Preference functions for PROMETHEE.

The available alternatives are assessed with respect to each criterion with the help of one of these preference functions. Usual, U-shape and Level functions are commonly used for qualitative criteria usually including a small number of levels. On the other hand, V-shape, Linear, and Gaussian are more suited for quantitative criteria.

These preference scores are then used to construct a pairwise comparison table for each criterion, as shown in the following (made-up) example:

For Criterion A

	A1	A2	A3
A1		1	1
A2	0		0.4
A3	0	0.3	

For Criterion B

	A1	A2	A3
A1		0.1	0
A2	0.6		0
A3	1	0.9	

Then the overall preference degree for each pair of alternatives is simply the weighted sum of their scores for all the individual criteria. In the above-mentioned example, we can obtain the following scores from the above-mentioned two tables if both Criterion A and Criterion B have equal weights:

Overall preference degree

	A1	A2	A3
A1		$(1 + 0.1)/2 = \mathbf{0.55}$	$(1 + 0)/2 = \mathbf{0.5}$
A2	$(0 + 0.6)/2 = \mathbf{0.3}$		$(0.4 + 0)/2 = \mathbf{0.2}$
A3	$(0 + 1)/2 = \mathbf{0.5}$	$(0.3 + 0.9)/2 = \mathbf{0.6}$	

This information can be used to calculate preference flows for each alternative. The average of each row (excluding diagonal elements) determines the positive outflow, denoted as φ^+, while the average of each column (excluding diagonal elements) determines the negative outflow, denoted as φ^-. These two values can be combined to calculate the net flow:

$$\varphi(a) = \varphi^+(a) - \varphi^-(a)$$

Using these calculations, we can obtain the following outflows (Table 7.1) for our example.

Looking at the net flows in Table 7.1, A2 is clearly dominated by the other two as the overall negative outflow is higher than the positive outflow. We can also argue that A3 is the most feasible option due to the fact that it has the highest value for net flow.

Table 7.1   Positive outflows, negative outflows and net flows.

	φ^+	φ^-	φ
A1	0.525	0.400	0.125
A2	0.250	0.575	− **0.325**
A3	0.550	0.350	0.200

In the above example, we find a negative correlation between the two outflows which is quite common and expected in a sense that those options having higher positive outflows somehow implies that they have better scores than those of other options, however, note that the positive outflows and negative outflows need not be perfectly correlated.

7.1   Theme Park

Mingliff is a growing city with a high influx of young working families in recent years. Your company, ThemeCons, is a well reputed consulting company for theme park development and has recently been contacted by Mingliff city council for their plans to build a theme park for the city dwellers and also to attract more tourists. The main challenge is to choose the most appropriate location for the theme park. After the initial survey and the screening process, ThemeCons and the council have shortlisted four sites for the theme park and choosing the most appropriate out of these four seems to be a hard exercise.

Economically, Site A appears to be highly feasible as it is nearest to the main population of Mingliff so it can attract a high number of visitors with the park itself used for marketing purposes as it will be visible from the river bank.

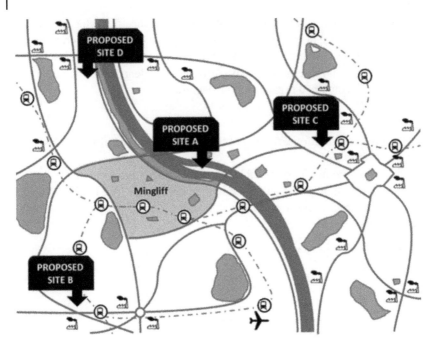

Figure 7.2 Understanding the geographic situation of Mingliff.

Technically, site A is difficult and costly to develop as some part will have to be extended over water. Electricity, water, and sewage needs to be arranged on the uninhabited island. Also, this site is not considered good for the environment as this will affect the aquatic life and risks contaminating the water due to increased vehicular traffic on roads and waters. Moreover, there are concerns in the community over the visual pollution disturbing the natural view from the river bank. The other three sites also come with their own sets of pros and cons, as summarised in Table 7.2.

The table describes the situation with respect to three important criteria of economic, technical, and environmental concerns. There are other important criteria of political, social, and legal concerns but all the four sites are more or less equal on those criteria and therefore they do not play any part in the decision-making exercise. In an attempt to quantify the available information, ThemeCons have translated the economic evaluations into return on investment and the technical evaluations into total duration of the project. For environmental concerns, they initially proposed to use carbon emissions but the emissions were not taking into account several different types of impact on the environment. Finally, they managed to obtain scores between 0 and 100 from expert evaluation where 0 implied devastating impact while 100 implied

Table 7.2 Summary of potential theme park sites pros and cons.

	Economic	Technical	Environmental
Site A	★★★★★	★	★
	Within town boundaries; high market, ease of access	Lots of extra work needed to extend on water	Water and visual pollution
Site B	★★★★	★	★★★★
	Strong connection to rail links and next to airport	Lots of extra work needed for rocky surface	A small impact on the existing plantation in nearby area
Site C	★★★	★★	★★★★★
	Away from population but has rail and road links	Extra work required for demolishing a few buildings	Almost no damage to the environment
Site D	★★	★★★★	★★★
	Away from population, no rail link	Existing infrastructure can be reused	Some deforestation will occur

no adverse impact at all. Whilst assessing the sites, the experts were also consulted for the thresholds of indifference and strict preference with respect to each of the three criteria. Table 7.2 was therefore translated with the help of these expert evaluations into Table 7.3.

Based on this quantification, ThemeCons calculated preference strengths for each pair of options with respect to all three criteria. Since all three criteria were quantitative they preferred using the linear preference function and obtained the scores as mentioned in Table 7.4.

Table 7.3 Expert evaluations.

	Economic	Technical	Environmental
Site A	14.20%	37 months	15 / 100
Site B	12.70%	30 months	45 / 100
Site C	12.20%	25 months	75 / 100
Site D	9.80%	16 months	30 / 100
w	**45%**	**30%**	**25%**
q	0.5%	2	5 / 100
p	1.5%	8	25 / 100

Table 7.4 Preference strengths.

Economic	A	B	C	D
A	0.00	1.00	1.00	1.00
B	0.00	0.00	0.50	1.00
C	0.00	0.00	0.00	1.00
D	0.00	0.00	0.00	0.00

Technical	A	B	C	D
A	0.00	1.00	1.00	1.00
B	0.00	0.00	0.83	1.00
C	0.00	0.00	0.00	1.00
D	0.00	0.00	0.00	0.00

Environmental	A	B	C	D
A	0.00	0.00	0.00	0.00
B	1.00	0.00	0.00	0.75
C	1.00	1.00	0.00	1.00
D	0.75	0.00	0.00	0.00

ThemeCons consulted the city council for the relative importance of the three main criteria in their assessments. The council gave the economic criterion the highest relative importance of 45% as they're a growing city and according to them, any opportunity for economic growth must be tapped into. The environmental criterion was considered less important but they cannot ignore it due to the environment-friendly population and the environmental regulations in place. They have assigned 30% importance to technical and 25% importance to the environmental criterion.

Using this information on the relative importance of the three criteria, ThemeCons managed to combine these partial scores into a set of aggregate scores, as below:

	A	B	C	D
A		0.75	0.75	0.75
B	0.25		0.48	0.94
C	0.25	0.25		1
D	0.19	0	0	

This information was then used to calculate the positive outflow (average of the row) as shown below in the right-most column and the negative outflow (the average of the column) for each location, as shown on the bottom row:

	A	B	C	D	
A		0.75	0.75	0.75	**0.75**
B	0.25		0.48	0.94	**0.55**
C	0.25	0.25		1	**0.50**
D	0.19	0	0		**0.06**
	0.23	**0.33**	**0.41**	**0.90**	

And eventually, they calculated the net flow for these locations by subtracting the negative outflow from the positive one:

	φ^+	φ^-	φ
A	0.750	0.230	**0.520**
B	0.554	0.330	**0.220**
C	0.500	0.410	**0.090**
D	0.062	0.900	**- 0.830**

These net flows gave an insight to ThemeCons to understand that Location D was the least feasible option for constructing a theme park, while Location A was the most feasible one as it dominated all other options.

7.2 PROMETHEE in Excel

Let us see how ThemeCons can use Excel to investigate the four sites using PROMETHEE. Recall how they translated the information from Table 7.2 into Table 7.3. The information in Table 7.3 can be the starting point for implementing PROMETHEE-based analysis in Excel, as shown in Figure 7.3 where assessment scores for each site are recorded for each criterion along with the criteria weights, indifference, and preference thresholds.

These assessment scores can be translated into a preference dominance relationship with the linear preference function, which was chosen for this problem earlier. In order to calculate the preference dominance relationship, we first calculate the difference of scores for every pair of options with respect to all the three criteria (economic, technical, and environmental), as shown in Figure 7.4. For example, see cell I4 for calculating the difference between the Site B score and the Site A score in economic criterion. The two referenced scores can be seen in Figure 7.3 at B6 and B5, respectively.

	A	B	C	D
1				
2		**Quantification by experts**		
3		*Economic*	*Technical*	*Environmental*
4	*units*	*return on investments*	*duration in months*	*0 to 100 scale*
5	*Site A*	14.20%	37	15
6	*Site B*	12.70%	30	45
7	*Site C*	12.20%	25	75
8	*Site D*	9.80%	16	30
9	*w*	45%	30%	25%
10	*q*	0.5%	2	5
11	*p*	1.5%	8	25

Figure 7.3 Data entry for PROMETHEE in Excel.

	H	I	J	K	L
1					
2	Economic	A	B	C	D
3	A	0.0%	1.5%	2.0%	4.4%
4		=$B6-$B$5	0.0%	0.5%	2.9%
5	C	-2.0%	-0.5%	0.0%	2.4%
6	D	-4.4%	-2.9%	-2.4%	0.0%
7					
8	Technical	A	B	C	D
9	A	0	7	12	21
10	B	-7	0	5	14
11	C	-12	-5	0	9
12	D	-21	-14	-9	0
13					
14	Environmental	A	B	C	D
15	A	0	-30	-60	-15
16	B	30	0	-30	15
17	C	60	30	0	45
18	D	15	-15	-45	0

Figure 7.4 Calculating the difference in scores for each pair of sites.

Now that the differences are calculated, we can clip those differences to 1 that exceeds the preference threshold p, and similarly, we can also clip those differences to 0 that happen to be smaller than the indifference threshold, q. This can be seen in Figure 7.5 which shows the IF expression in cell I22 to

	H	I	J	K	L
19					
20	Economic	A	B	C	D
21	A	0.00	1.00	1.00	1.00
22	=IF((I4-$B$10)/($B$11-		0.00	0.00	1.00
23	$B$10)<0, 0, IF((I4-		0.00	0.00	1.00
24	$B$10)/($B$11-$B$10)>		0.00	0.00	0.00
25	1, 1, (I4-$B$10)/($B$11-				
26	$B$10)))		B	C	D
27	IF(logical_test, [value_if_true], [value_if_false])			1.00	1.00
28	B	0.00	0.00	0.50	1.00
29	C	0.00	0.00	0.00	1.00
30	D	0.00	0.00	0.00	0.00
31					
32	Environmental	A	B	C	D
33	A	0.00	0.00	0.00	0.00
34	B	1.00	0.00	0.00	0.50
35	C	1.00	1.00	0.00	1.00
36	D	0.50	0.00	0.00	0.00
37					
38					

Figure 7.5 Calculating preference dominance using linear function.

calculate the dominance relation for site B over site A. Note the presence of two nested IF statements, where outer IF is testing for indifference threshold and the inner IF statement is testing for preference threshold. If the value remains within the two thresholds, it is simply retained without modification.

So far, we have calculated the preference dominance relations for each criterion separately. An overall (or aggregate) preference relation can simply be calculated using the weighted average of these individual values. Figure 7.6 demonstrates how we can calculate the weighted average of individual criterion-level scores to obtain an overall preference dominance value.

	A	B	C	D	E
13		Preference degree			
14		A	B	C	D
15	A		0.70	0.75	0.75
16	=I22*$B$9+I28*$C$9+I34*$D$9			0.15	0.88
17	C	0.25	0.25		1.00
18	D	0.13	0.00	0.00	

Figure 7.6 Adding criterion-level scores to calculate overall preference dominance.

In order to calculate the positive outflow, we take the row average for each site, and similarly, to calculate the negative outflow we take the column average for each site, as shown in Figure 7.7.

	A	B		C	D	E	F
13		Preference degree					
14		A		B	C	D	
15	A			0.70	0.75	0.75	0.73
16	B	0.25			0.15	0.88	0.43
17	C	0.25		0.25		1.00	0.50
18	D	0.13		0.00	0.00		0.04
19		=AVERAGE(B15:B18)		0.32	0.30	0.88	

Figure 7.7 Calculating -ve outflow (use row average for +ve outflow).

The net flow for each site can easily be calculated by subtracting negative outflow from the positive outflow, as demonstrated in Figure 7.8 for site A by subtracting C21 from B21 which turns out to be 0.53, making site A the most appropriate amongst the four sites, as mentioned earlier.

	A	B	C	D
20		positive flow	negative flow	net flow
21	A	0.73	0.21	=B21-C21
22	B	0.43	0.32	0.11
23	C	0.50	0.30	0.20
24	D	0.04	0.88	-0.83

Figure 7.8 Calculating net flow for each site.

7.3   PROMETHEE in R

Install the MCDA package and library:

```
install.packages("MCDA")
install.library("MCDA")
```

Create a decision matrix called Scores:

```
scores<-rbind( c(0.142, 37, 15),
        c(0.127, 30, 45),
        c(0.122, 25, 75),
        c(0.098, 16, 30) )
rownames(scores) <- c("Site-A","Site-B","Site-C","Site-D")
colnames(scores) <- c("Economic","Technical","Environm
ental")
```

Set the values for q, p, w, g, and minmax:

```
q<-c(0.005, 2, 5)
```

```
names(q)<-colnames(scores)
p<-c(0.015, 8, 25)
names(p)<-colnames(scores)
w<-c(0.45, 0.30, 0.25)
names(w)<-colnames(scores)
g<-c(4, 0, 0)
names(g)<-colnames(scores)
minmax<-c("max","min","max")
names(minmax)<-colnames(scores)
pref_func <- c("Usual","Usual","Usual")
names(pref_func)<-colnames(scores)
```

Use the PROMETHEE function to calculate the results:

```
res <- PROMETHEEI(scores, pref_func, p, q, g, w, minmax)
print(res)
res1 <- PROMETHEEII(scores, pref_func, p, q, g, w, minmax)
print(res1)
```

7.4 Further Problems to Test Your PROMETHEE Skills

Now that you have mastered PROMETHEE methods in Excel and R why don't you try to solve the following two problems. The solutions to the problems are available on our accompanying website:

http://www.smartdecisionsbook.com

1) You are judging a cake competition and want to decide who will get the bronze, silver and gold awards. You want to judge the three cakes on the following criteria all marked on a scale 1 to 5: taste, design, and skill. You have also assigned criteria weights (w), indifference thresholds (q), and preference thresholds (p).

	Cake A	Cake B	Cake C
Design	3.6	4.1	3.5
Taste	4.5	4.2	3.8
Skill	3.2	3.5	4.8
w	25	50	25
q	0.1	0.1	0.1
p	0.3	0.2	0.5

Which cakes take gold, silver, and bronze?

2) You are changing electricity provider and have four companies to choose from. You are taking into consideration the amount of renewable energy the company provides (%), price (£), and customer service rating (/10). You have also assigned criteria weights (w), indifference thresholds (q), and preference thresholds (p).

	Renewable	Price	Customer service
Company A	80	17.2	8
Company B	100	20.5	8
Company C	95	16.9	3
Company D	60	17	9
w	60	30	10
q	5	0.5	1
p	10	1.2	3

Considering all the factors which electricity company should you go for?

8

Goal Programming

Most people have life goals such as becoming financially secure, having a family, travelling around the world, owning a dream house, learning another language or starting one's own company. Yet, we all have limited resources such as money, time, health, and skills. Therefore, we must be realistic and for most this means translating these goals into constraints. For example, we may want to see every capital city in the world but due to money and time we usually limit our travelling to a few days'/weeks' holiday per year. This happens due to the fact we have multiple objectives to achieve where one objective is often in conflict with another (e.g., wanting to become financially secure requires time and effort which restricts us from travelling the globe). Although our objectives and constraints appear different at a first glance, many objectives can be translated into constraints. This is what we do in goal programming in order to strike the right balance between multiple objectives.

Goal programming has been around since the 1950s[1] and can be used to solve problems with more than one overall measure of performance (i.e., problems with multiple objectives). It has been used to address problems relating to accounting, energy forecasting, portfolio management, water resource management, diet planning, police scheduling, engineering, and manufacturing.[2] It is generally regarded as an adaptation of linear programming and is sometimes referred to as multi-objective linear programming. It works by minimising an achievement function that represents a mathematical expression of unwanted deviation variables. The deviation variables represent how far you have positively or negatively deviated away from your goals. This sounds complicated but you'll see from the example that it's really quite easy to understand and simple to use.

---

1 Although it was used in the 1950s it was first named in Charnes, A., and Cooper, W.W. (1961). *Management Models and Industrial Applications of Linear Programming*. New York: Wiley.

2 According to Tamiz, M., Jones, D.F., and El-Darzi, E. (1995). A review of goal programming and its applications. *Annals of Operations Research* 58 (1).

Smart Decisions: A Structured Approach to Decision Analysis Using MCDA, First Edition.
Edited by Richard Edgar Hodgett, Sajid Siraj, and Ellen Louise Hogg.
© 2024 John Wiley & Sons Ltd. Published 2024 by John Wiley & Sons Ltd.

There are different extensions of goal programming that have emerged which have become very popular such as Weighted Goal Programming and Lexicographic Goal Programming. Weighted goal programming (which is also known as Archimedean goal programming) allows for weights to be assigned to each of your goals so that differences in their importance can be modelled. Lexicographic goal programming (which is also known as pre-emptive goal programming) is generally used when there are major differences in the importance of goals. It works by putting goals into an order of importance and then ensuring that the most important goals are met first. This chapter will show you how to use the original version of goal programming and both the weighted and lexicographic variants.

8.1 Select How Many Products to Manufacture Using Goal Programming in Excel

A toy company can make three different types of toy robot (A, B, and C) as shown in Figure 8.1. The company wants to work out what is the best number of each toy to make per day. The company makes £11, £16, and £8 profit for a single sale of toy A, toy B, and toy C respectively. However, it takes a production line 20 minutes to make one unit of toy A, 12 minutes to make a one unit of toy B, and 40 minutes to make one unit of toy C. Furthermore, due to new regulations, the toys have to come supplied with batteries which are purchased from an external supplier. Toy A requires 4 batteries, toy B requires 3 batteries, and toy C requires 6 batteries.

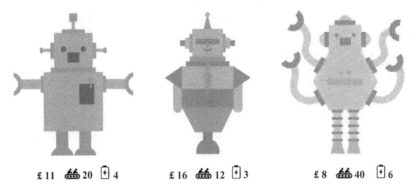

£ 11 🔧 20 🔋 4   £ 16 🔧 12 🔋 3   £ 8 🔧 40 🔋 6

Figure 8.1   Three different types of toy robot.

The company wants to make at least £1000 profit per day but only has 1200 minutes of production line labour available per day. The company does not want to lose any staff (i.e., does not want less than 1200 minutes of labour a day) but also does not want to pay overtime. In addition, due to flooding the company's battery supplier have said they can only deliver 200 batteries per day while they replenish their stock.

These three goals can be represented as simple equations where A, B, and C are the number of toy A, B, and C to produce respectively:

Labour: $20A + 12B + 40C \pm$ deviations $= 1200$
Profit: $11A + 16B + 8C \pm$ deviations $= 1000$
Batteries: $4A + 3B + 6C \pm$ deviations $= 200$

You will notice that deviations are present for each of the goals. As it is unlikely that there is a perfect combination of A, B, and C which meet all of the goals, deviations are used in the equations to allow some movement away from the goals. In goal programming we use an optimisation algorithm to minimise these deviations with the aim to identify a solution as close to the goals as possible.

In this example we are going to use Excel Solver to help select the best number of toy robots to make. If you haven't used Excel Solver before it is likely you need to enable it in Excel. To do this click on File (on the top left), click Options then open the Add-ins menu from the tab on the left. At the bottom of the screen select to manage Excel Add-Ins then click Go as shown in Figure 8.2.

Then as shown in Figure 8.3, tick the box for the Solver Add-in and click OK.

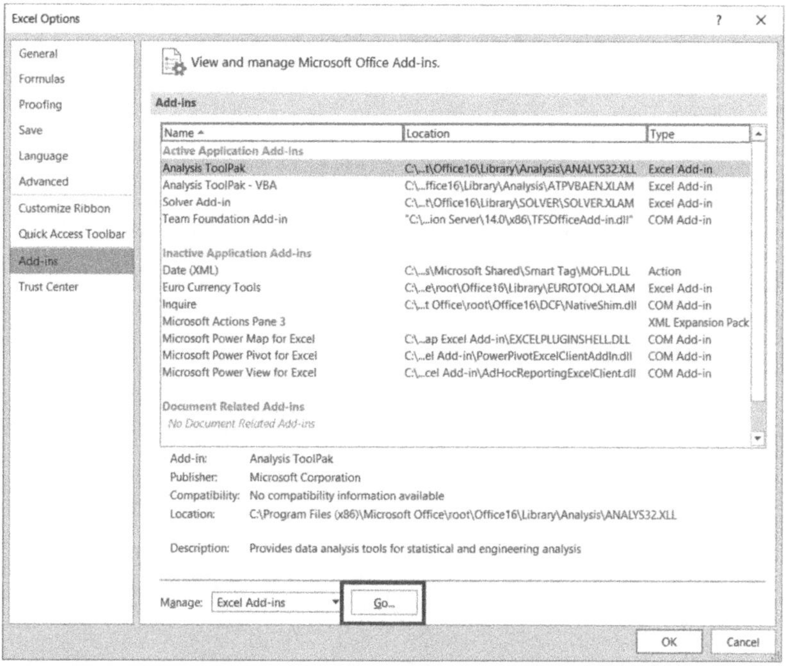

Figure 8.2 How to navigate to the Excel Add-Ins menu.

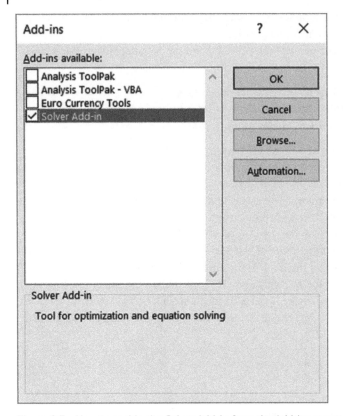

Figure 8.3 How to enable the Solver Add-in from the Add-ins menu.

To check that it has been enabled properly, click on the Data tab and Solver should now be available on the right under the Analyze section (as shown in Figure 8.4).

Figure 8.4 Data menu with Solver.

Before we can use Solver we need to set up the Excel spreadsheet. First, create a new Excel spreadsheet and enter a table with the goals, number of toys, deviations, targets, lower bounds, and variables as shown in Figure 8.5.

	A	B	C	D	E	F	G	H	I	J	K	L	M
1													
2						Labour		Profit		Batteries			
3			TOY A	TOY B	TOY C	+	-	+	-	+	-	Equals	Goal
4		Labour	20	12	40	-1	1						1200
5		Profit	11	16	8			-1	1				1000
6		Batteries	4	3	6					-1	1		200
7													
8		Lower Bounds:	0	0	0	0	0	0	0	0	0		
9													
10		Variables:	0	0	0	0	0	0	0	0	0		
11													

Figure 8.5 Spreadsheet designed for solving the toy selection problem.

As you will see there are two deviations for each goal (+ and -) which allow for positive and negative deviations away from your goals. There are two columns named Equals and Goal which will be used to match the calculated values for each of the goals to the goal targets. There are also two rows named Lower Bounds and Variables. The variable cells are the cells which Excel Solver will adjust with the aim to find the best solution and the lower bound cells will be used to set lower bounds for each of the variables so that Excel Solver doesn't identify a negative number of toys or deviations.

We need to add a formula to the Equals cells to calculate values for the goals. In cell L4 enter the following formula:

=SUMPRODUCT(C4:K4,C$10:K$10)

This will sum the total of each of the variables multiplied by the values and deviation variables related to labour. You can simply drag the bottom right of this cell down by two cells to add the formula related to profit and batteries. You will notice that under the positive deviation away from labour there is a -1 in the table. This is necessary so that the SUMPRODUCT formula in the Equals column can equal the Goal. For example, the positive deviation away from labour needs to be multiplied by -1 so that the Equals column matches the goal.

The final cell to add to the spreadsheet is to store the objective function, this is the function which Solver will attempt to minimise. To do this, add the following formula to cell C12: **=SUM(F10:K10)**

Your spreadsheet should now look like Figure 8.6.

	A	B	C	D	E	F	G	H	I	J	K	L	M
1													
2						Labour		Profit		Batteries			
3			TOY A	TOY B	TOY C	+	-	+	-	+	-	Equals	Goal
4		Labour	20	12	40	-1	1					0	1200
5		Profit	11	16	8			-1	1			0	1000
6		Batteries	4	3	6					-1	1	0	200
7													
8		Lower Bounds:	0	0	0	0	0	0	0	0	0		
9													
10		Variables:	0	0	0	0	0	0	0	0	0		
11													
12	Objective Function:		0										
13													

Figure 8.6 Spreadsheet with formula inserted into the Equals column.

Now we are ready to configure Excel Solver. Click on the Data tab then on the Solver button.

A form will appear (as shown in Figure 8.7) where you can set your objective function, changing variable cells, and add constraints. Set the objective to the

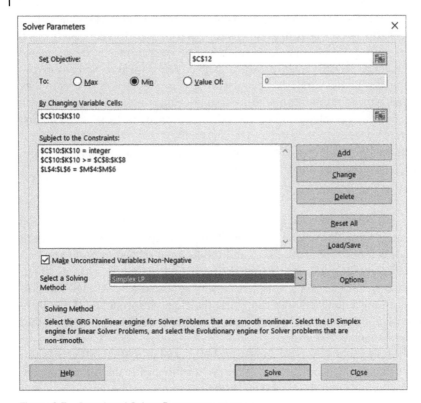

Figure 8.7 Completed Solver Parameters menu.

objective function cell (C12) and set the objective to Min (minimise). Then set the Changing Variable Cells to the variable cells (C10:K10).

Now we need to add a few constraints:

- Click on the Add button and set the Equals cells (L4:L6) to equal (=) the Goal cells (M4:M6) then click OK.
- Click on the Add button and set the variable cells (C10:K10) to be larger or equal (≥) to the lower bound cells (C8:K8).
- Click on the Add button and set the variable cells (C10:K10) to integer (int).

Finally select Simplex LP as the solving method and then you are ready to press Solve.

After a few seconds a Solver Results screen will appear. Select Keep Solver solution and press OK.

You will notice that the Objective Function, Equals and Variable values will have updated showing the solution shown in Figure 8.8.

		TOY A	TOY B	TOY C	Labour +	Labour -	Profit +	Profit -	Batteries +	Batteries -	Equals	Goal
	Labour	20	12	40	-1	1					1200	1200
	Profit	11	16	8			-1	1			1000	1000
	Batteries	4	3	6					-1	1	200	200
	Lower Bounds:	0	0	0	0	0	0	0	0	0		
	Variables:	1	55	13	0	0	0	5	47	0		
Objective Function:	52											

Figure 8.8 Solution for the toy selection problem.

The proposed solution is to manufacture 1 of Toy A, 55 of Toy B, and 13 of Toy C. This solution however has two deviations; requiring 47 more batteries and getting £5 less profit. You can easily see where these numbers come from by calculating the number of toys produced against profits and batteries. For example, with respect to profits you have (1×£11) + (55×£16) + (13×£8) = £995 which is £5 less than the £1000 goal.

This version of goal programming assumes that every deviation has an equal importance but in most scenarios this is not the case. For example, the toy manufacturer may not be as concerned about meeting their labour and battery goals as they are about meeting their profit goal. Furthermore, I'm pretty sure any sensible business would be much more concerned about achieving less profit than achieving more profit than their goal. This is where weighted and Lexicographic Goal Programming comes in.

First let's try Weighted Goal Programming which only requires a few quick modifications to our spreadsheet. First we need to add some weights for our deviation variables as shown in Figure 8.9.

		TOY A	TOY B	TOY C	Labour +	Labour -	Profit +	Profit -	Batteries +	Batteries -	Equals	Goal
	Labour	20	12	40	-1	1					1200	1200
	Profit	11	16	8			-1	1			1000	1000
	Batteries	4	3	6					-1	1	200	200
	Lower Bounds:	0	0	0	0	0	0	0	0	0		
	Variables:	1	55	13	0	0	0	5	47	0		
Objective Function:	52		Weights:	5	1	1	10	10	1			
			Normalised Weights:									

Figure 8.9 Spreadsheet with weights added for Weighted Goal Programming.

The negative deviation variable for profit and the positive deviation variable for batteries have been given a relatively high weight indicating a high importance. The positive deviation variable for labour has been given a medium weight and the remaining deviations have been given low weights.

You will notice that we have added a Normalised Weights row below Weights. This is because we need to normalise the weights as each goal has a different unit of measurement (hours, £, and number of batteries). The easiest normalisation method is percentage normalisation where each deviation is turned into a percentage value away from its goal. In cell F13 place the following formula:

=F12/M4

This divides the penalty value (5) by the goal for labour (1200). Do this for each of the weight cells:

G13:= G12/M4J13:=J12/M6
H13:=H12/M5K13:=K12/M6
I13:=I12/M5

Next we need to update the objective function to incorporate the weights into the calculation.

Select the objective function cell and update the formula to:

=SUMPRODUCT(F13:K13,F10:K10)

Then you can open Excel Solver and press the Solve button. This will provide a new solution based on the weighted importance of the deviation variables as shown in Figure 8.10.

					Labour		Profit		Batteries			
		TOY A	TOY B	TOY C	+	-	+	-	+	-	Equals	Goal
	Labour	20	12	40	-1	1					1200	1200
	Profit	11	16	8			-1	1			1000	1000
	Batteries	4	3	6					-1	1	200	200
	Lower Bounds:	0	0	0	0	0	0	0	0	0		
	Variables:	1	61	2	0	368	3	0	0	1		
Objective Function:	0.314667			Weights:	5	1	1	10	10	1		
				Normalised Weights:	0.004167	0.000833	0.001	0.01	0.05	0.005		

Figure 8.10 Solution for the toy selection problem using Weighted Goal Programming.

This time the solution is to produce 1 of Toy A, 61 of Toy B, and 2 of Toy C. There are three deviations for this scenario which are to have 368 hours less labour time, £3 more profit and 1 less battery. When using the Solver function in Excel the Solver works to meet the constraints set to minimise the objective function. The Solver returns the first result where all the constraints have been satisfied and can find the local minimum and may not find the global minimum in some circumstances. Therefore, it is possible for the Solver to return slightly different results to the ones shown.

Now, what if one of the goals becomes much more important than the rest? For example, if your battery supplier was unable to increase the supply of 200 batteries delivered every day and your insurance company doesn't allow you to store batteries at the workshop overnight meaning you must meet the 200 battery limit goal. This is where Lexicographic Goal Programming becomes very useful.

Let's remove our weights used in Weighted Goal Programming and the objective function. Unlike using the original and weighted versions of goal programming where you have one objective function and use Solver once to find a solution, Lexicographic Goal Programming is carried out in multiple steps. The first step is to create your first priority level setting which deviation variables are the most important as shown in Figure 8.11.

	A	B	C	D	E	F	G	H	I	J	K	L	M	N
1														
2						Labour		Profit		Batteries				
3			TOY A	TOY B	TOY C	+	-	+	-	+	-	Equals	Goal	
4		Labour	20	12	40	-1	1					0	1200	
5		Profit	11	16	8			-1	1			0	1000	
6		Batteries	4	3	6					-1	1	0	200	
7														
8		Lower Bounds:	0	0	0	0	0	0	0	0	0			
9														
10		Variables:	0	0	0	0	0	0	0	0	0			
11													Objective Functions	
12				Priority 1:	0	0	0	0	1	0				
13														

Figure 8.11   Spreadsheet with a priority level for Lexicographic Goal Programming.

As you can see, the positive deviation for batteries has been set as the most important deviation. In the objective function (cell M12) insert the following formula:

> =SUMPRODUCT(F10:K10,F12:K12)

Now open Solver and set the objective function to cell M12 and press solve. You will find a solution where the positive deviation variable for Batteries is 0 as shown in Figure 8.12.

	A	B	C	D	E	F	G	H	I	J	K	L	M	N
1														
2						Labour		Profit		Batteries				
3			TOY A	TOY B	TOY C	+	-	+	-	+	-	Equals	Goal	
4		Labour	20	12	40	-1	1					1200	1200	
5		Profit	11	16	8			-1	1			1000	1000	
6		Batteries	4	3	6					-1	1	200	200	
7														
8		Lower Bounds:	0	0	0	0	0	0	0	0	0			
9														
10		Variables:	6	58	0	0	384	0	6	0	2			
11													Objective Functions	
12				Priority 1:	0	0	0	0	1	0			0	
13														

Figure 8.12   Solution for first priority of Lexicographic Goal Programming.

Now we can add a second priority level which sets the negative deviation for batteries as the second most important deviation as shown in Figure 8.13.

For the objective function (cell M13) insert:

> =SUMPRODUCT(F10:K10,F13:K13)

	A	B	C	D	E	F	G	H	I	J	K	L	M	N
1														
2							Labour		Profit		Batteries			
3			TOY A	TOY B	TOY C	+	-	+	-	+	-	Equals	Goal	
4		Labour	20	12	40	-1	1					1200	1200	
5		Profit	11	16	8			-1	1			1000	1000	
6		Batteries	4	3	6					-1	1	200	200	
7														
8	Lower Bounds:		0	0	0	0	0	0	0	0	0			
9														
10	Variables:		6	58	0	0	384	0	6	0	2			
11													Objective Functions	
12					Priority 1:	0	0	0	0	1	0		0	
13					Priority 2:	0	0	0	0	0	1			
14														

Figure 8.13 Spreadsheet with a second priority level for Lexicographic Goal Programming.

Now open Solver and set the objective function to cell M13 then add a constraint to set cell J10 (the positive deviation for batteries) to 0 as shown in Figure 8.14.

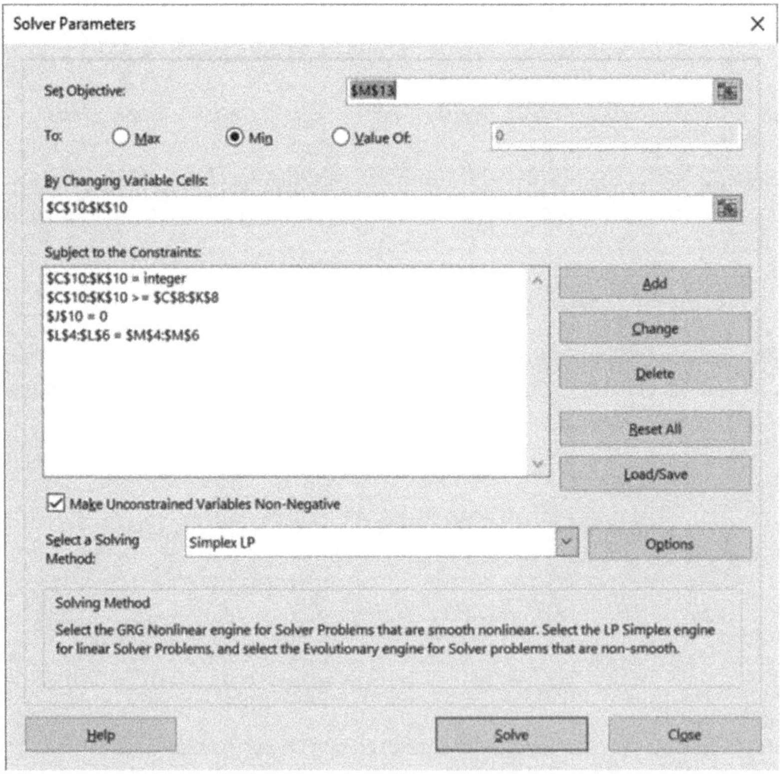

Figure 8.14 Solver parameters for the second priority level.

After pressing Solve you should now have a solution where both the positive and negative deviations for batteries are 0 as shown in Figure 8.15.

	TOY A	TOY B	TOY C	Labour +	Labour -	Profit +	Profit -	Batteries +	Batteries -	Equals	Goal
Labour	20	12	40	-1	1					1200	1200
Profit	11	16	8			-1	1			1000	1000
Batteries	4	3	6					-1	1	200	200
Lower Bounds:	0	0	0	0	0	0	0	0	0		
Variables:	50	0	0	0	200	0	450	0	0		
										Objective Functions	
			Priority 1:	0	0	0	0	1	0	0	
			Priority 2:	0	0	0	0	0	1	0	

Figure 8.15 Solution for second priority of Lexicographic Goal Programming.

This solution shows that profit has been reduced, let's set this deviation as the next priority as shown in Figure 8.16.

	TOY A	TOY B	TOY C	Labour +	Labour -	Profit +	Profit -	Batteries +	Batteries -	Equals	Goal
Labour	20	12	40	-1	1					1200	1200
Profit	11	16	8			-1	1			1000	1000
Batteries	4	3	6					-1	1	200	200
Lower Bounds:	0	0	0	0	0	0	0	0	0		
Variables:	50	0	0	0	200	0	450	0	0		
										Objective Functions	
			Priority 1:	0	0	0	0	1	0	0	
			Priority 2:	0	0	0	0	0	1	0	
			Priority 3:	0	0	0	1	0	0	0	

Figure 8.16 Spreadsheet with a third priority level for Lexicographic Goal Programming.

Set the objective function (cell M14) to:

=SUMPRODUCT(F10:K10,F14:K14)

Then open up Solver, set the objective function to cell M14 and add a new constraint setting cell K10 to 0 as shown in Figure 8.17.

This gives a solution where the negative deviation for profit is 0 as shown in Figure 8.18.

Let's add one more priority for the negative deviation for labour as we don't want to have to let anyone go! This is shown in Figure 8.19.

Set the objective function (cell M15) to:

=SUMPRODUCT(F10:K10,F15:K15)

Then open Solver and set the objective function to cell M15 and add a new constraint setting cell I10 to 0. This gives us a new solution (as shown in Figure 8.20) but unfortunately the negative deviation for labour hasn't been reduced to 0. Instead it has been lowered to 376 resulting in an increase in profits to 22.

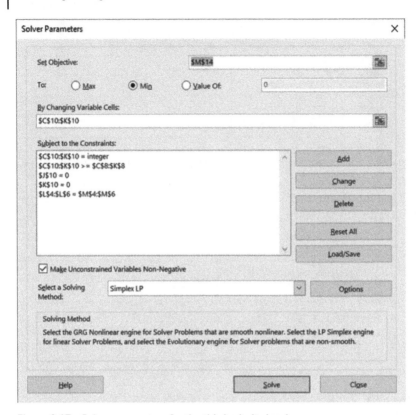

Figure 8.17 Solver parameters for the third priority level.

Figure 8.18 Solution for third priority of Lexicographic Goal Programming.

As you can see using Lexicographic Goal Programming in Excel is quite laborious in comparison to the original and weighted variants. Therefore, the next section will focus on how to quickly model Lexicographic Goal Programming in R.

	A	B	C	D	E	F	G	H	I	J	K	L	M	N
1														
2						Labour		Profit		Batteries				
3			TOY A	TOY B	TOY C	+	-	+	-	+	-	Equals	Goal	
4		Labour	20	12	40	-1	1					1200	1200	
5		Profit	11	16	8			-1	1			1000	1000	
6		Batteries	4	3	6					-1	1	200	200	
7														
8		Lower Bounds:	0	0	0	0	0	0	0	0	0			
9														
10		Variables:	5	60	0	0	380	15	0	0	0			
11													Objective Functions	
12					Priority 1:	0	0	0	0	1	0		0	
13					Priority 2:	0	0	0	0	0	1		0	
14					Priority 3:	0	0	0	1	0	0		0	
15					Priority 4:	0	1	0	0	0	0			
16														

Figure 8.19 Spreadsheet with a fourth priority level for Lexicographic Goal Programming.

	A	B	C	D	E	F	G	H	I	J	K	L	M	N
1														
2						Labour		Profit		Batteries				
3			TOY A	TOY B	TOY C	+	-	+	-	+	-	Equals	Goal	
4		Labour	20	12	40	-1	1					1200	1200	
5		Profit	11	16	8			-1	1			1000	1000	
6		Batteries	4	3	6					-1	1	200	200	
7														
8		Lower Bounds:	0	0	0	0	0	0	0	0	0			
9														
10		Variables:	2	62	1	0	376	22	0	0	0			
11													Objective Functions	
12					Priority 1:	0	0	0	0	1	0		0	
13					Priority 2:	0	0	0	0	0	1		0	
14					Priority 3:	0	0	0	1	0	0		0	
15					Priority 4:	0	1	0	0	0	0		376	
16														

Figure 8.20 Solution for fourth priority of Lexicographic Goal Programming.

8.2 Select How Many Products to Manufacture Using Goal Programming in R

The easiest way to utilise goal programming in R is to use the fantastic goalp package developed by Dr. David Palma at the University of Leeds.

You can install the package using: install.packages("goalp")
Then you can add the package to your R library using: library("goalp")

Next, we need to input the problem:

```
problem  <-"Labour :    20*A + 12*B + 40*C = 1200
            Profit:     11*A + 16*B + 8*C = 1000
            Batteries: 4*A + 3*B + 6*C = 200"
```

Finally, we solve the problem and get the results using:

```
solution <- goalp(problem)
summary(solution)
```

It's as simple as that. You will see the results are the same as we calculated in Excel; 1 of Toy A, 55 of Toy B, and 13 of Toy C with deviations required for profit and batteries.

It's just as easy to use weighted and Lexicographic Goal Programming with the goalp package.

For Weighted Goal Programming, we add the weights but normalise them (in the same way we did in Excel).

```
wproblem <- "Labour:      20*A + 12*B + 40*C = 1200 |
                          1/12005/1200
            Profit:      11*A + 16*B + 8*C = 1000 | 10/1000
                          1/1000
            Batteries:   4*A +  3*B + 6*C = 200 |
                          1/20010/200"
wsolution <- goalp(wproblem)
summary(wsolution)
```

You will see the results are the same as we calculated in Excel. For Lexicographic Goal Programming we provide the priority levels after #, so #1 would be the first priority, #2 would be the second priority and (in this example) #5 would be the joint last priority:

```
lproblem <- "Labour :    20*A + 12*B + 40*C = 1200 | #4 #5
             Profit:     11*A + 16*B + 8*C = 1000 | #3 #5
             Batteries:  4*A + 3*B + 6*C = 200 | #2 #1"
lsolution <- goalp(lproblem)
summary(lsolution)
```

Again, you will see the results are exactly the same as we calculated in Excel.

8.3   Further Problems to Test Your Goal Programming Skills

Now that you have mastered goal programming methods in Excel and R why don't you try to solve the following two problems. The solutions to the problems are available on our accompanying website:

http://www.smartdecisionsbook.com

1) A mobile phone manufacturer makes two types of mobile phones, the x-phone and the z-phone. The company makes £60 profit per x-phone and £75 profit per z-phone. It takes the employees 1 hour to make an x-phone and 2 hours to make a z-phone and there are 500 hours of labour available per day. To make an x-phone requires two memory chips while a z-phone requires four memory chips. There is a shortage of memory chips at the moment and the company can only get 1000 chips delivered per day.

The company does not want to lose any staff (does not want less than 500 hours of labour a day) but also doesn't want to pay overtime.

The company wants to make at least £20 000 profit per day and can only use 1000 memory chips per day.

How many x-phone and z-phone mobile phones would you recommend the company to produce per day?

Do you have to make any compromises to make your recommended number of mobile phones?

2) A furniture company makes three different types of chairs, A, B, and C. The company makes £40, £55, and £60 profit for the sale of chair A, chair B, and chair C respectively.

It takes the carpenters 20 minutes to make a single chair A, 30 minutes to make a single chair B, and 25 minutes to make a single chair C. There are 1000 minutes of carpenter labour available per day.

The carpenters use four brackets to make a single Chair A or B and six brackets to make a single chair C. 150 brackets are delivered to the company each day.

The company does not want to lose any staff (does not want less than 1000 minutes of labour a day) but also doesn't want to pay overtime.

The company wants to make at least £2000 profit per day and only use 150 brackets per day.

How many of each chair model would you recommend the company to produce per day?

Do you have to make any compromises to make your recommended number of chairs?

9

Evolutionary Optimisation

9.1 European Road Trip

This year Richard (one of the super amazing book authors) is planning to travel around Europe in his old worn out campervan with his wife Louise and two dogs, Guinness and Snoopy:

Figure 9.0 Guinness and Snoopy in the campervan.

Smart Decisions: A Structured Approach to Decision Analysis Using MCDA, First Edition.
Edited by Richard Edgar Hodgett, Sajid Siraj, and Ellen Louise Hogg.
© 2024 John Wiley & Sons Ltd. Published 2024 by John Wiley & Sons Ltd.

Together Richard and Louise have identified eight European cities they would like to visit and intend on starting and finishing their journey from Calais to allow them to get the Eurotunnel from the UK. The only thing is, they want to travel the shortest distance to get to all of the cities. We will use a genetic algorithm to search for the best route to take. This type of problem is often called the travelling salesman problem where a salesman needs to find a tour of cities where each city is visited once and the shortest distance is travelled.

9.2 Model the European Road Trip in Excel

To start we need to list the cities Richard and Louise want to visit. Create a new Excel spreadsheet and in cells A2:A10 list the following cities:

- Calais
- Prague
- Ljubljana
- Belgrade
- Budapest
- Gdansk
- Bansko
- Munich
- Split

The first cell should contain the start and end point which for Richard and Louise is Calais. Next we need to create a distance matrix that contains data on all of the distances between each of the cities. In cells C1:K1 and B2:B10 places the numbers 1 to 9 then fill the diagonal values with 0 so your sheet should now look like Figure 9.1.

Now we need to add all of the distances to the matrix, there are many ways to do this but one simple (but unfortunately time consuming) way is by using Google maps as shown in Figure 9.2.

	A	B	C	D	E	F	G	H	I	J	K	L
1			1	2	3	4	5	6	7	8	9	
2	Calais	1	0									
3	Prague	2		0								
4	Ljubljana	3			0							
5	Belgrade	4				0						
6	Budapest	5					0					
7	Gdansk	6						0				
8	Bansko	7							0			
9	Munich	8								0		
10	Split	9									0	
11												

Figure 9.1 Distance matrix with cities to visit.

Figure 9.2 Identifying distances between cities using Google Maps.

The distances between two cities needs to be sought in both directions as the distances are not exactly the same in each direction due to one way systems and the placement of slip roads. Once complete you should have a distance matrix that looks something like Figure 9.3.

This matrix contains all the driving distances between all of the cities listed in kilometres. Next we need to input a random travel order, in cells C12:K12 insert the numbers 1 to 9 then in cell L12 insert the number 1. Next we need to input the distances between the cities below the travel order, to do this input the following formula into cell C13:

$$=INDEX(\$C\$2:\$K\$10,C12,D12)$$

Then you can drag the bottom right corner of cell C13 to cell K13. Now we need to sum the total distance travelled, in cell C15 input the following formula:

$$=SUM(C13:K13)$$

Your sheet should now look something like Figure 9.4.

Now we can configure Solver to find the shortest distance using a Genetic Algorithm. Open Solver from the Data tab. If the Solver button isn't there, don't panic! Take a look at Section 8.1 which shows you how to add it. Once the Solver window opens, set the objective as cell C15 (the total distance travelled) and set the objective to minimise (we want the shortest distance). Set the changing variables as C12:K12 then we need to add two constraints:

- Set cell L12 to equal cell C12 as shown in Figure 9.5a. This forces the end destination to be the same as the start.
- Set cells C12:K12 to different by selecting *dif* in the dropdown box as shown in Figure 9.5b.

A	B	C	D	E	F	G	H	I	J	K	L
1		1	2	3	4	5	6	7	8	9	
2 Calais	1	0	1090	1380	1912	1552	1461	2443	972	1815	
3 Prague	2	1091	0	653	899	532	738	1430	362	1033	
4 Ljubljana	3	1379	652	0	533	462	1287	1064	405	468	
5 Belgrade	4	1912	896	531	0	378	1317	534	939	545	
6 Budapest	5	1551	525	463	379	0	938	910	655	750	
7 Gdansk	6	1460	791	1289	1327	1029	0	1858	1120	1669	
8 Bansko	7	2442	1425	1060	533	908	1846	0	1468	1004	
9 Munich	8	971	360	406	938	654	1119	1469	0	873	
10 Split	9	1848	1033	467	550	750	1668	1005	875	0	
11											

Figure 9.3 Completed distance matrix.

	A	B	C	D	E	F	G	H	I	J	K	L	M
1			1	2	3	4	5	6	7	8	9		
2	Calais	1	0	1090	1380	1912	1552	1461	2443	972	1815		
3	Prague	2	1091	0	653	899	532	738	1430	362	1033		
4	Ljubljana	3	1379	652	0	533	462	1287	1064	405	468		
5	Belgrade	4	1912	896	531	0	378	1317	534	939	545		
6	Budapest	5	1551	525	463	379	0	938	910	655	750		
7	Gdansk	6	1460	791	1289	1327	1029	0	1858	1120	1669		
8	Bansko	7	2442	1425	1060	533	908	1846	0	1468	1004		
9	Munich	8	971	360	406	938	654	1119	1469	0	873		
10	Split	9	1848	1033	467	550	750	1668	1005	875	0		
11													
12	Travel Order:		1	2	3	4	5	6	7	8	9	1	
13			1090	653	533	378	938	1858	1468	873	1848		
14													
15	Distance Travelled:		9639	km									

Figure 9.4 Distance matrix with random travel order added.

(a)

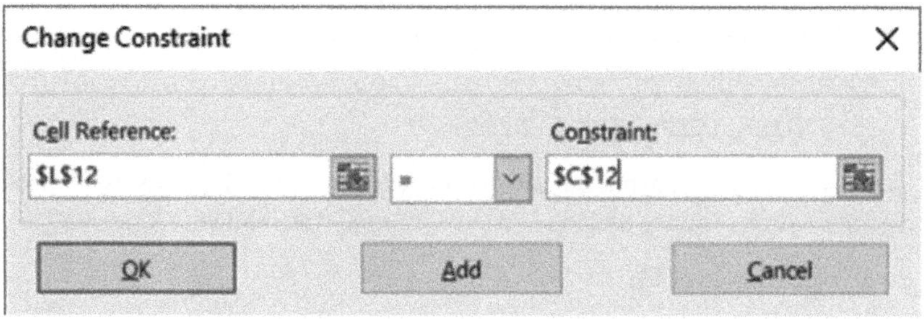

(b)

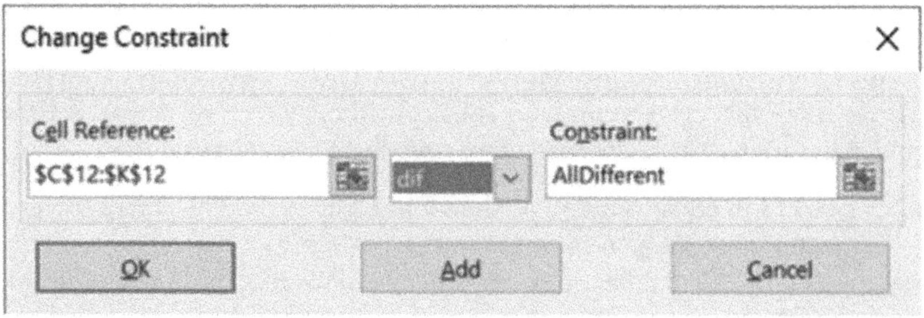

Figure 9.5 Constraints to add.

Then set the solving method to Evolutionary (which uses a genetic algorithm) as shown in Figure 9.6 then click on the Options button and select the Evolutionary tab.

In the evolutionary tab you can set the Genetic Algorithm parameters. Change the Maximum time without improvement to 10 seconds as shown in

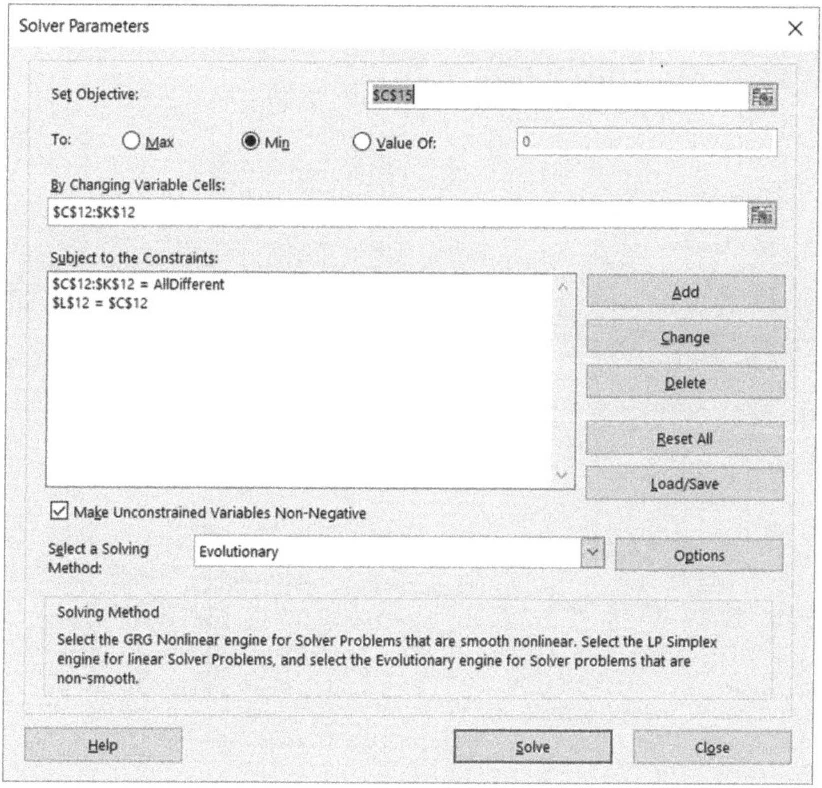

Figure 9.6 Solver settings.

Figure 9.7 and click OK. Just in case you were wondering what the other parameters mean, they are explained below (see Table 9.1):

Now click Solve and you will notice the text at the bottom of the screen shows the number of iterations increasing and (hopefully) the objective function lowering over time. Eventually the Genetic Algorithm will finish its search and present you with the Solver Results window as shown in Figure 9.8.

When you click OK you will see the travel order has updated and the new total distance travelled is displayed as shown in Figure 9.9.

As you can see in Figure 9.10, the genetic algorithm has found a solution that looks like a circular route.

Figure 9.7 Evolutionary settings for solver.

Table 9.1 Explanation of evolutionary parameters.

Convergence	This is the percentage difference in objective values for the top 99% of the population that Solver should allow in order to stop. Lower values will usually attain a solution closer to the optimal solution but will require more time.
Mutation Rate	As explained earlier, the mutation rate sets the randomness of the search. Set this higher to increase the stochastic nature (randomness) of the search and lower to reduce it.
Population Size	How many data points the genetic algorithm uses for searching at the same time.
Random Seed	This allows you to set a fixed seed for the randomness in the algorithm. If you set this, you will get the same result as others who use the same seed values. If you leave this blank a different random seed will be used each time. The seed needs to be a positive whole number.
Maximum Time Without Improvement	The maximum number of seconds you want the Solver to continue searching without meaningful improvement in the objective function value.

Solver Results   ×

Solver cannot improve the current solution. All
Constraints are satisfied.   Re**p**orts

⊙ **K**eep Solver Solution   Answer
                                                    Population
○ **R**estore Original Values

☐ Re**t**urn to Solver Parameters Dialog   ☐ O**u**tline Reports

| OK | **C**ancel | | **S**ave Scenario... |

Solver cannot improve the current solution. All Constraints are satisfied.

When the Evolutionary engine is used, this means Solver stopped because it can not find a better solution in
the given time.

Figure 9.8   Solver results window.

11											
12	Travel Order:	1	8	3	9	7	4	5	2	6	1
13		972	406	468	1005	533	378	525	738	1460	
14											
15	Distance Travelled:	6485	km								
16											

Figure 9.9   Updated travel order and total distance.

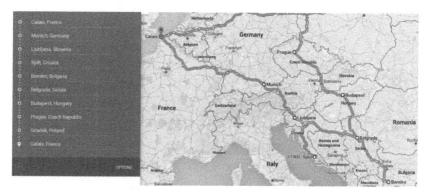

Figure 9.10   Solution route to travel.

9.3 Model the European Road Trip in R

A function for Genetic Algorithm isn't available in the base package of R but there are many packages available which you can install and add to your R library. One of the best is the ga() function in the GA package written by Professor Luca Scrucca at the University of Perugia. This package can be used for permuting, i.e. arranging the decision variables into a sequence of order. For a travelling salesman type problem this works really well. To install this package use install.packages("GA") then use library("GA") to add this package to your R library.

Next we need to create a function which will calculate the distance of a tour of cities that can be optimised using the ga() function. The function for this is below and it may look a little complicated at first but it's actually quite straightforward. The function has been split into five steps. Have a read through the function then take a look at the explanation for each of the steps below:

```
calcdist <- function(tour)
{
# STEP 1: Add start and end position (1) to our tour and
increase all other values by 1
tour <- c(1, tour+1, 1)
# STEP 2: Given a tour create a route
route <- embed(c(tour, 1), 2)[, 2:1]
# STEP 3: Create a distance matrix called dist
dist <- matrix(c(0, 1090, 1380, 1912, 1552, 1461, 2443,
972, 1815, 1091, 0, 653, 899, 532, 738, 1430, 362,
1033, 1379, 652, 0, 533, 462, 1287, 1064, 405, 468,
1912, 896, 531, 0, 378, 1317, 534, 939, 545, 1551, 525,
463, 379, 0, 938, 910, 655, 750, 1460, 791, 1289, 1327,
1029, 0, 1858, 1120, 1669, 2442, 1425, 1060, 533, 908,
1846, 0, 1468, 1004, 971, 360, 406, 938, 654, 1119,
1469, 0, 873, 1848, 1033, 467, 550, 750, 1668, 1005,
875, 0), nrow=9, ncol=9, byrow = TRUE)

# STEP 4: Calculate distance travelled on route
totaldist <- sum(dist[route])

# STEP 5: Return the total distance as a negative
return(-totaldist)
}
```

Step 1	As the ga() function searches for a permutation, the decision variables need to be ordered from 1 to the number of cities visited. To force the tour to start at 1 and end at 1 we can modify the tour given by the genetic algorithm. As the tour given by the genetic algorithm will have 1 in it, we can increase the values in the tour by 1.
	So for example, the ga evaluates the tour 5-4-3-1-2-7-6-8
	Our code changes this tour to: 1-6-5-4-2-3-8-7-9-1 which is applicable to our problem.
Step 2	At the moment we have a series of numbers which represents our tour. To format these numbers in a way which we can calculate all of the distances in the tour we can convert the tour to a route (a list of routes to travel as start and end positions).
	For example, if we convert the 1-6-5-4-2-3-8-7-9-1 tour to a route, we get:
	[,1] [,2]
	[1,] 1 6
	[2,] 6 5
	[3,] 5 4
	[4,] 4 2
	[5,] 2 3
	[6,] 3 8
	[7,] 8 7
	[8,] 7 9
	[9,] 9 1
Step 3	We need to input all of the distances between the cities. Similarly to what we did in the Excel solution we store these in a distance matrix.
Step 4	Now we calculate the total distance travelled using the route and distance matrix.
Step 5	We now have the total distance travelled and we need the function to return this so the optimiser can evaluate its input. As the ga() function maximises (finds the largest value) and we want to find the minimum (shortest) distance, we simply return the negative of the distance.

Now that we have a function to optimise, we can use the ga() function with:

```
result <- ga(type = "permutation", fitness = calcdist,
min=1, max=8)
```

This sets the ga() function to search for a permutation using the objective function calcdist and sets the lowest number of permutation to 1 and the highest to 8. We can then view the summary of the optimisation using summary(result). However, the solution given in this summary needs to

```
> route
 [1] 1 8 3 9 7 4 5 2 6 1
>
```

Figure 9.11 Solution found using R.

be updated as we updated the order of our tour in Step 1 of the function above. To get the true result use: `route <- c(1, result@solution+1, 1)` then call back `route`.

You will see the result given in Figure 9.11 is identical to the result found in Excel.

9.4 Further Problems to Test Your Evolutionary Optimisation Skills

Now that you have mastered evolutionary optimisation methods in Excel and R why don't you try to solve the following two problems. The solutions to the problems are available on our accompanying website: http://www. smartdecisionsbook.com

1. You are take some friends on a guided tour of parks in Leeds. To keep your guests happy you want to minimise the time driving in the car. These are the parks you wish to visit:
   1) Roundhay Park
   2) Golden Acre Park
   3) Temple Newsham Park
   4) Woodhouse Moor
   5) Burley Park
   6) Potternewton Park
   7) Meanwood Park
   8) Farnley Hall Park
   9) Middleton Park

   What order should you visit the parks to minimise time in the car, starting and ending the trip at Roundhay park?

2. A shipping company wants to optimise the order that they load their ship. The ship will set sail from Southampton, UK and wants to load containers so that the first port they visit is packed last and the last port they visit is packed first. The company wants to sail the minimum total distance between all the ports.

Container 1 – Antwerp, Belgium
Container 2 – Gdansk, Poland
Container 3 – Rotterdam, Netherlands
Container 4 – Dublin, Ireland
Container 5 – Brindisi, Italy
Container 6 – Calais, France
Container 7 – Kavala, Greece
Container 8 – Lisbon, Portugal

In what order should the containers be packed?

10

Dealing with Uncertainty

Dealing with risk and uncertainty is a huge part of decision-making. It is rare that you can collect all the information you need to model a decision with complete certainty. Some decisions are going to be more uncertain than others. The examples we have used in the previous chapters generally have a low amount of uncertainty, it is unlikely the prices of cars or distances of houses are going to be incorrect or change. However, many personal decisions or decisions faced in industry will have high amounts of uncertainty as data are not available or it is difficult to provide an accurate score.

Due to the importance of dealing with uncertainty, many methods and variations of methods have been proposed to handle uncertainty. The most common approach has been to adopt fuzzy based approaches. Fuzzy set theory was proposed in the 1960s.[1] Before then, logic was simply defined by two values, 1 or 0 and was termed crisp logic with an object being an element of a set or not. Fuzzy logic alternatively introduces the concept of membership. This is easiest to explain with an example. Let's say we wanted to provide definitions of warm and hot. As we live in the United Kingdom, people would say that anything over 15 °C outside is warm and anything over 20 °C is hot. So, a crisp definition of warm could be between 15 and 19.9 °C and hot between 20 °C and 24.9 °C. Therefore, if it is 19 °C outside, the temperature would be classified as warm (i.e., warm = 1 and hot = 0). Fuzzy logic works differently, using membership. Figure 10.1 shows an example representation of fuzzy sets for warm and hot where warm is between 13 °C and 22 °C with only 17.5 °C being at a membership of 1 and hot is between 18 °C and 27 °C with only 22.5 °C being at a membership of 1.

With the example in Figure 10.1, if it was 19 °C outside, the temperature would have a 0.7 membership of warm and 0.2 membership of hot meaning the most likely classification is warm. To get the membership values, you draw

---

1 L.A.Zadeh (1965). "Fuzzy Sets". *Information and control* 8(3):338–353.

Smart Decisions: A Structured Approach to Decision Analysis Using MCDA, First Edition.
Edited by Richard Edgar Hodgett, Sajid Siraj, and Ellen Louise Hogg.
© 2024 John Wiley & Sons Ltd. Published 2024 by John Wiley & Sons Ltd.

a line up from the bottom axis and see where it intersects with the triangles for warm and hot on the left axis. Fuzzy logic has been applied to most multi-Criteria decision analysis techniques to capture uncertainty, for example, there are published methods for fuzzy AHP and fuzzy TOPSIS while ELECTRE III already incorporates fuzzy logic.

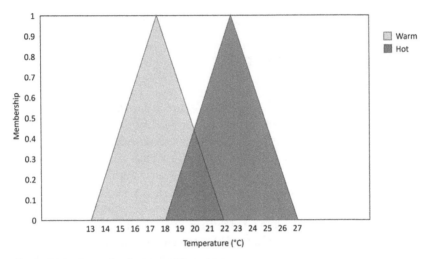

Figure 10.1 Example of crisp and fuzzy logic.

Another well-known method for dealing with uncertain information is Multi-Attribute Utility Theory (MAUT) which was primarily designed to handle trade-offs among multiple criteria for a given situation. It requires the selection of utility functions which represent the risk attitude of the decision-maker for each criterion in a decision problem. It has been extensively discussed in the decision-making literature and is generally valued for its axiomatic foundations. However, MAUT is also known to be difficult to use in practice as it specifies uncertain outcomes by means of probability distributions which are not typically known. As a result, there are few real-world examples of MAUT being used in academic literature in comparison to its theoretical development.

A more recent method proposed in 2019 for assisting decision-makers in the presence of high levels of uncertainty is Simulated Uncertainty Range Evaluations (SURE).[2] SURE has evolved from an existing method that has been applied extensively in the pharmaceutical and speciality chemical sectors. The new method

---

2 R.E.Hodgett and S. Siraj (2019). "SURE: A method for decision-making under uncertainty". Expert systems with Applications, (115): 684–694.

utilises simulations based upon triangular distributions to create a plot which visualises the preferences and overlapping uncertainties of decision alternatives. It facilitates decision-makers to visualise the not-so-obvious uncertainties of decision alternatives. This is the method we will be focusing on in this chapter.

The SURE methodology uniquely requires the decision-maker to provide three scores for each alternative with respect to each criterion where there is uncertainty. These scores represent the most likely values, the lowest possible values, and the highest possible values. If a value is certain, then that single value is sufficient to represent all three (minimum, most likely, and maximum) values. This information is used along with simulations based upon triangular distributions to generate many decision tables. The number of simulations to use (and number of decision tables created) depends on the size of the problem but in most cases 10 000 simulations would be enough and only takes a few seconds to calculate on a modern computer. These simulated decision tables are normalised, and the results are calculated with the weighted sum method. The results are then presented in the form of a density plot. An overview of the process is shown in Figure 10.2 and is summarised by the following five steps:

1) Set the number of decision tables to be simulated.
2) Generate this number of simulated decision tables using the minimum, most likely, and maximum values as the input parameters to the triangular distributions.
3) Normalise decision tables using summation ratio normalisation (see Table 3.3).
4) Calculate the results of the simulated decision tables using the weighted sum method.
5) Plot the results using a kernel density plot.

SURE can very easily be implemented in R but is a little more challenging in Excel as there is not currently an Excel function available for generating numbers based on triangular distributions or functionality for plotting kernel density plots. Therefore, you will learn to use a VBA function to handle the triangular distributions in Excel. We will also make a compromise to display the output of SURE in the form of a frequency distribution. There are add-on software packages for Excel that can support creating kernel density plots, but we will not cover this as you will learn how to easily do this in R.

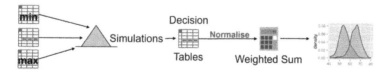

Figure 10.2 Overview of the SURE method.

10.1   Select the Best Way to Cut Down a Tree in Excel

Shane recently bought a new house (using the methods taught in this book) and is incredibly happy with it but there is one problem he needs to solve. There is a rotten tree in the back garden that blocks light from the area where he likes to sit and read about decision-making. He hasn't cut down a tree before but is determined to do it himself. He does a little research online and finds three viable ways to cut down the tree; using a chainsaw, an axe or a handsaw. He also identifies three criteria that are important to him. The first is cost as he doesn't own any equipment for cutting down a tree, the second is time as he doesn't want to give up too much of his weekend working on this and the third is safety as he definitely doesn't want to injure himself.

The chainsaw is the quickest option, but they are expensive to buy especially if you include safety equipment and due to the rotating blades, it is the least safe method. The axe will take a lot of physical exertion so is a slower method, but it is cheaper to purchase even if we include maintenance such as sharpening the blade. It is also safer than the chainsaw but there is still the potential to swing the axe and miss the tree. The hand saw will require the most physical exertion and will take the longest time to cut down the tree, but it is the cheapest to buy even if we need multiple blades and it is also the safest option. Shane creates the decision table in Table 10.1 to help make his decision. He is uncertain about many of the values so has provided minimum, maximum, and most likely values for each alternative with respect to each criterion. He has also weighted safety as the most important criterion followed by cost and time.

Table 10.1 Decision table for using SURE to select a method for cutting down a tree.

	Cost (minimising)			Time (minimising)			Safety (maximising)		
Weight	60			20			100		
	Mini-mum	Most Likely	Maxi-mum	Mini-mum	Most Likely	Maxi-mum	Mini-mum	Most Likely	Maxi-mum
Chainsaw	120	120	120	20	20	40	1	3	6
Axe	28	30	50	120	140	160	3	6	7
Handsaw	10	15	20	120	180	250	9	9	10

To start modelling this problem in Excel, you need to create a new Excel Macro Enabled Workbook. To do this, open Excel and then select File then Save As. Directly below where you enter the filename, you will have an option for Save as Type. In this drop-down box, select Excel Macro Enabled Workbook. Once your file is saved, enter the details in Table 10.1 into Excel as shown in Figure 10.3.

A	B	C	D	E	F	G	H	I	J	K
1										
2			Cost			Time			Safety		
3			(minimising)			(minimising)			(maximising)		
4	Weight:		60			20			100		
5		Minimum	Most Likely	Maximum	Minimum	Most Likely	Maximum	Minimum	Most Likely	Maximum
6	Chainsaw	120	120	120	20	20	40	1	3	6
7	Axe	28	30	50	120	140	160	3	6	7
8	Handsaw	10	15	20	120	180	250	9	9	10

Figure 10.3 Decision in the in Excel.

Before we start simulating decision tables, we need to inverse the minimising scores and normalise the criteria weights. To do this copy the table in B2:K8 into B12:K18 and amend all the values associated with the minimising criteria (Cost and Time) to have the inverse of values in the first table. For example, in cell C16 enter:

=C6^-1

To normalise the weights, we need to divide each weight by the total, so for cell C14 enter:

=C4/SUM($C$4:$K$4)

You can drag this across to the right to give the normalised weights for all three criteria. You should now have a worksheet that looks like Figure 10.4.

A	B	C	D	E	F	G	H	I	J	K
1										
2			Cost			Time			Safety		
3			(minimising)			(minimising)			(maximising)		
4	Weight:		60			20			100		
5		Minimum	Most Likely	Maximum	Minimum	Most Likely	Maximum	Minimum	Most Likely	Maximum
6	Chainsaw	120	120	120	20	20	40	1	3	6
7	Axe	28	30	50	120	140	160	3	6	7
8	Handsaw	10	15	20	120	180	250	9	9	10
9										
10	Inverse minimising scores & normalise weights									
11										
12			Cost			Time			Safety		
13										
14	Weight:		0.333333333			0.111111111			0.555555556		
15		Minimum	Most Likely	Maximum	Minimum	Most Likely	Maximum	Minimum	Most Likely	Maximum
16	Chainsaw	0.008333333	0.008333	0.008333	0.05	0.05	0.025	1	3	6
17	Axe	0.035714286	0.033333	0.02	0.008333	0.007143	0.00625	3	6	7
18	Handsaw	0.1	0.066667	0.05	0.008333	0.005556	0.004	9	9	10
19										

Figure 10.4 Table with all maximising scores and normalised weights.

Now comes the tricky part, to generate simulated decision tables using triangular distributions we need to use some VBA macro magic to create a new Excel function to use. If you are using Windows, you need to hold down Alt and press F11 and if you are using a Mac you need to press Opt + F11 to bring up the VBA interface. Next you need to click on Insert and select Module. This will bring up a window for you to enter Visual Basic code. You need to enter the code shown in Figure 10.5.

```
Function RTri(Minimum As Double, Mode As Double, Maximum As Double) As Double
    Dim LowerRange As Double, HigherRange As Double, TotalRange As Double, CumulativeProb As Double, Test As Boolean

    Application.Volatile

    Test = False
    If Minimum = Mode Then
        If Mode = Maximum Then
            Test = True
        End If
    End If

    If Test = False Then
        LowerRange = Mode - Minimum
        HigherRange = Maximum - Mode
        TotalRange = Maximum - Minimum
        CumulativeProb = Rnd()
        If CumulativeProb < (LowerRange / TotalRange) Then
            RTri = Minimum + Sqr(CumulativeProb * LowerRange * TotalRange)
        Else
            RTri = Maximum - Sqr((1 - CumulativeProb) * HigherRange * TotalRange)
        End If
    Else
        RTri = Mode
    End If
End Function
```

Figure 10.5 VBA code used to generate random numbers based on the triangular distribution.

This code may look very confusing, especially if you haven't come across Visual Basic before but don't worry. All this code is doing is creating a function that requires three inputs; the minimum, most likely (mode) and maximum values. It then checks to see if all the values are the same and if so, returns that value. This means for values where there is certainty (like the cost of a chainsaw, that is 120 for all three values) the value remains the same. If the values aren't the same, a random number based on the three values provided is generated and returned.

Once you have entered the code, click save and return to the Excel workbook. Now you will be able to use a brand-new function called RTri. To keep each simulated table on a single row which we can drag down to replicate, enter the headings shown in Figure 10.6.

		Cost			Time			Safety	
19									
20 Simulations using VBA function									
21									
22		Cost			Time			Safety	
23	Chainsaw	Axe	Handsaw	Chainsaw	Axe	Handsaw	Chainsaw	Axe	Handsaw
24									

Figure 10.6 Table for simulations.

In Cell C24, you can now use the RTri function to generate a random number based on the minimum, most likely, and maximum values for the cost of a chainsaw by entering:

=RTri($C$16,$D$16,$E$16)

As all the numbers provided are the same (0.008333333), the function will return 0.008333333.

In Cell D24, you can enter:

=RTri($C$17,$D$17,$E$17)

This will generate a random number for the cost of an axe. You will now have a table that looks like Figure 10.7 however the number you have for axe will likely be a bit different (as it is random!).

Use the RTri function to create random numbers for all the alternatives with respect to all criteria. You should now have a workbook that looks like Figure 10.8 with you first simulated decision table.

	A	B	C	D	E	F	G	H	I	J	K
19											
20	Simulations using VBA function										
21											
22				Cost			Time			Safety	
23			Chainsaw	Axe	Handsaw	Chainsaw	Axe	Handsaw	Chainsaw	Axe	Handsaw
24			0.008333333	0.036716							
25											

Figure 10.7 Simulations for chainsaw and axe with regards to cost.

	A	B	C	D	E	F	G	H	I	J	K
1											
2				Cost			Time			Safety	
3				(minimising)			(minimising)			(maximising)	
4		Weight:		60			20			100	
5			Minimum	Most Likely	Maximum	Minimum	Most Likely	Maximum	Minimum	Most Likely	Maximum
6		Chainsaw	120	120	120	20	20	40	1	3	6
7		Axe	28	30	50	120	140	160	3	6	7
8		Handsaw	10	15	20	120	180	250	9	9	10
9											
10	Inverse minimising scores & normalise weights										
11											
12				Cost			Time			Safety	
13											
14		Weight:		0.333333333			0.111111111			0.555555556	
15			Minimum	Most Likely	Maximum	Minimum	Most Likely	Maximum	Minimum	Most Likely	Maximum
16		Chainsaw	0.008333333	0.008333	0.008333	0.05	0.05	0.025	1	3	6
17		Axe	0.035714286	0.033333	0.02	0.008333	0.007143	0.00625	3	6	7
18		Handsaw	0.1	0.066667	0.05	0.008333	0.005556	0.004	9	9	10
19											
20	Simulations using VBA function										
21											
22				Cost			Time			Safety	
23			Chainsaw	Axe	Handsaw	Chainsaw	Axe	Handsaw	Chainsaw	Axe	Handsaw
24			0.008333333	0.006911	0.04014	0.00251	0.009175	0.010492	3.583013	4.876794	9.208741
25											
26											

Figure 10.8 Workbook with first simulated decision table.

Before we go on to drag this down and create many simulated tables, we need to add a way of normalising this information and calculating the results. First, we can copy the simulations table text (in cells C22:K23) and paste it to the right (to cells M22:U23). Then we can add titles for the results in W23:Y23, containing chainsaw, axe, and handsaw.

In Cell M24, as shown in Figure 10.9, we can add:

=$C24/SUM($C24:$E24)

Add all the formula needed to cells M24:U24 to normalise the simulated decision table. Finally, we can add the following to cells W24:Y24 to calculate the results for the first simulated table:

W24: **=($M24*$C$14)+($P24*$F$14)+($S24*$I$14)**
X24: **=($N24*$C$14)+($Q24*$F$14)+($T24*$I$14)**
Y24: **=($O24*$C$14)+($R24*$F$14)+($U24*$I$14)**

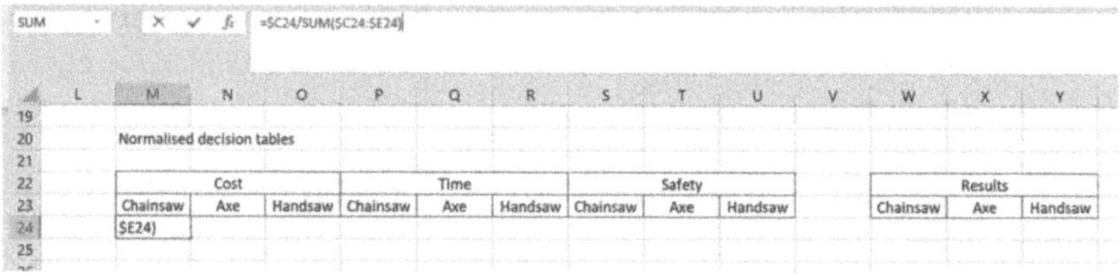

Figure 10.9 Normalising the first generated decision table.

Now, it is just a case of dragging cells C24:Y24 down for the number of decision tables you would like to simulate. More simulations are better, but it can be slow to calculate depending on the specification of your computer. For this example, I have just generated 1000 simulated decision tables by dragging C24:Y24 down to C1023:Y1023.

If you scroll down the results shown in columns W, X, and Y. You should see that each row is very different but generally the handsaw has the highest score followed by the axe then the chainsaw. We should expect to see this in our results.

As mentioned previously, there isn't an easy way to create kernel density plots in Excel. So, for this example we are going to create a frequency distribution shown with a line or bar chart. This isn't ideal as kernel density plots are better at presenting a distribution's shape as they are not influenced by the number of bins used in a frequency distribution. It will however give us a good indication of each distribution's shape and you will see in the next section how easy it is to generate kernel density plots in R.

To start, create a new tab where we can put the data for creating a frequency distribution. The data needs to be separated into bins which we can plot. As the results are always going to be between 0 and 1, we can separate the data into 0.02 increments (i.e., 50 bins).

In cell B2 type the title Bin-Low and in C2 the title Bin-High, then under Bin-Low (in cells B3:B5) type the values 0.00, 0.02, and 0.04 and under Bin-High (in cells C3:C5) type 0.02, 0.04, and 0.06. You can then highlight the cells and drag them down until we have all 50 bins that we need as shown in Figure 10.10.

Now we need to calculate the frequency for each bin for each alternative. In Cells D2:F2, enter the names of the three alternatives: chainsaw, axe, and handsaw. Then below chainsaw (in D3), enter:

=COUNTIFS(SURE!W$24:W$1023,">"&$B3, SURE!W$24:W$1023,"
<"&$C3)

(where SURE!W$24:W$1023 is the location of the simulated results for chainsaw).

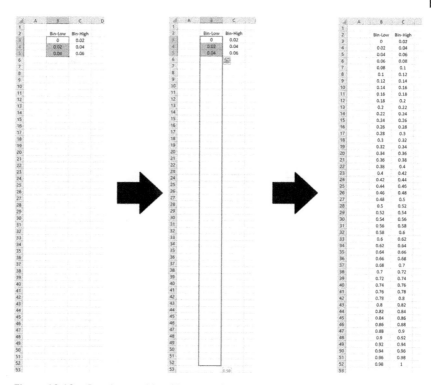

Figure 10.10 Creating a table of lower and upper bounds of 50 bins.

You can then drag this cell to the right to F3 and then select D3:F3 and drag it down to D52:F52 which will give you a table that looks like Figure 10.11 (although not exactly the same due to the random numbers used).

Now it is just a case of plotting the data. We can either do this with a line chart or a bar chart. Select D2:F52 then go to Insert and select Line Chart. You will now see the frequency distributions represented by lines. You will need to amend the x-axis to show the scores rather than the bin number. To do this, right click on the axis and click on Select Data, in the Select Data Source window, on the right-hand side, under Horizontal (Category) Axis labels, click Edit and select B3:B52 as the Axis label range. This will provide you with a chart that looks like Figure 10.12.

You can see from the results that the handsaw was clearly the best alternative followed by an axe then a chainsaw. You can see there is quite a bit of uncertainty overlap between the chainsaw and axe alternatives.

Let's also visualise the same information in the form of a bar chart. Again, select D2:F52 then go to Insert and instead this time, select Bar Chart. You will need to amend the x-axis again, just like you did with the line chart. This will provide you with a chart that looks like Figure 10.13.

	A	B	C	D	E	F
1						
2		Bin-Low	Bin-High	Chainsaw	Axe	Handsaw
3		0	0.02	0	0	0
4		0.02	0.04	0	0	0
5		0.04	0.06	0	0	0
6		0.06	0.08	7	0	0
7		0.08	0.1	29	0	0
8		0.1	0.12	69	0	0
9		0.12	0.14	145	0	0
10		0.14	0.16	207	3	0
11		0.16	0.18	217	13	0
12		0.18	0.2	177	68	0
13		0.2	0.22	89	134	0
14		0.22	0.24	43	214	0
15		0.24	0.26	17	193	0
16		0.26	0.28	0	160	0
17		0.28	0.3	0	100	0
18		0.3	0.32	0	56	0
19		0.32	0.34	0	28	0
20		0.34	0.36	0	12	0
21		0.36	0.38	0	11	0
22		0.38	0.4	0	7	0
23		0.4	0.42	0	0	1
24		0.42	0.44	0	1	1
25		0.44	0.46	0	0	6
26		0.46	0.48	0	0	21
27		0.48	0.5	0	0	19
28		0.5	0.52	0	0	48
29		0.52	0.54	0	0	85
30		0.54	0.56	0	0	113
31		0.56	0.58	0	0	114
32		0.58	0.6	0	0	183
33		0.6	0.62	0	0	175
34		0.62	0.64	0	0	138
35		0.64	0.66	0	0	61
36		0.66	0.68	0	0	28
37		0.68	0.7	0	0	7
38		0.7	0.72	0	0	0
39		0.72	0.74	0	0	0
40		0.74	0.76	0	0	0
41		0.76	0.78	0	0	0
42		0.78	0.8	0	0	0
43		0.8	0.82	0	0	0
44		0.82	0.84	0	0	0
45		0.84	0.86	0	0	0
46		0.86	0.88	0	0	0
47		0.88	0.9	0	0	0
48		0.9	0.92	0	0	0
49		0.92	0.94	0	0	0
50		0.94	0.96	0	0	0
51		0.96	0.98	0	0	0
52		0.98	1	0	0	0
53						

Figure 10.11 The results separated into bins, ready for plotting.

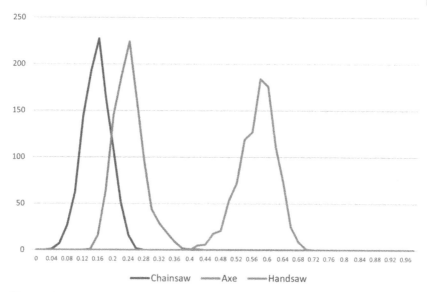

Figure 10.12   SURE results in Excel using a line chart.

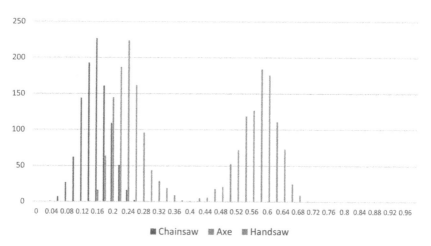

Figure 10.13   SURE results in excel using a bar chart.

You will see both charts look very similar, however a kernel density plot would provide a better representation of the densities than using a frequency distribution. You can however improve these plots by increasing the number of bins and increasing the number of simulations used.

10.2   Select the Best Way to Cut Down a Tree in R

So, let's model the exact same problem in R. To start open R and run the following to install the MCDA package for R and add the package to your R library:

```
install.packages("MCDA")
library("MCDA")
```

You will now be able to use the SURE function in the MCDA package. Next, we need to enter the data:

```
performanceTableMin <- matrix(c(120,28,10,20,120,120,
1,3,9),nrow=3,ncol=3, byrow=TRUE)
performanceTable <- matrix(c(120,30,15,20,140,180,3,6,
9),nrow=3,ncol=3, byrow=TRUE)
performanceTableMax <- matrix(c(120,50,20,40,160,250,
6,7,10),nrow=3,ncol=3, byrow=TRUE)

row.names(performanceTable) <-
c("Cost","Time","Safety")
colnames(performanceTable) <-
c("Chainsaw","Axe","Handsaw")
row.names(performanceTableMin) <- row.
names(performanceTable)
colnames(performanceTableMin) <-
colnames(performanceTable)
row.names(performanceTableMax) <- row.
names(performanceTable)
colnames(performanceTableMax) <-
colnames(performanceTable)

criteriaWeights <- c(60, 20, 100)
criteriaWeights <- criteriaWeights /
sum(criteriaWeights)
names(criteriaWeights) <- row.names(performanceTable)

criteriaMinMax <- c("min", "min", "max")
names(criteriaMinMax) <- row.names(performanceTable)
```

Now that all the data is entered, we can use the SURE function in the MCDA package for R to give us the results:

```
results <- SURE(performanceTableMin, performanceTable,
performanceTableMax, criteriaWeights, criteriaMinMax)
```

We can then plot the results using a kernel density plot with:

```
plotSURE(results)
```

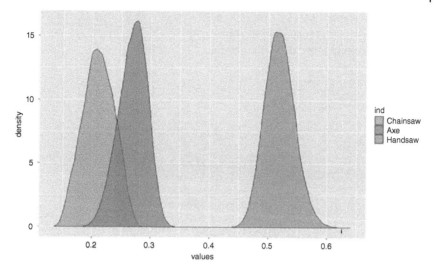

Figure 10.14 The output of SURE using R.

As you will see the results in R (shown in Figure 10.14) are similar to what we found in Excel, but the distributions have cleaner lines. The results in both Excel and R shown that the handsaw was the best alternative. There is overlap in the results for the axe and chainsaw but it is likely the axe will perform better.

10.3 Further Problems to Test Your SURE Skills

Now that you have mastered using SURE in Excel and R why don't you try to solve the following two problems. The solutions to the problems are available on our accompanying website:

http://www.smartdecisionsbook.com

10.3.1 Project Planning

The company you work for is in the early stages of expanding their clothing range. You have taken on the role of project manager and have been tasked to find the most attractive market to launch into next from sports clothing, lounge wear, and work wear.

The company has two criteria by which it wants the new markets judged. Competing brands in market and the number of retailers that would consider selling the company's products. They have been assigned the weights of

35 and 65 respectively. The range of possible values that the marketing team has collected can be seen in Figure 10.15.

Which clothing range do you recommend launching?

	A	B	C	D	E	F	G	H
1								
2		Competing Brands (minimising)			Retailers (maximising)			
3	Weights	35			65			
4		Minimum	Most likely	Maximum	Minimum	Most likely	Maximum	
5	Sports Clothing	60	80	100	10	15	50	
6	Lounge Wear	10	35	50	4	8	16	
7	Work Wear	30	45	70	5	9	30	
8								
9								
10								
11								
12								

Figure 10.15 Decision data for clothing market.

10.3.2 Taking a Job

You have been offered a new position at your current employer and at the same time you have received a job offer from a new employer. The details of the jobs are still to be confirmed but you need to reply to the first offer.

The criteria you have decided to judge the new job opportunities on are salary, job satisfaction (/10), and opportunities for promotion (/10). The range of possible values you have decided on can be seen in Figure 10.16.

Which job do you take?

	A	B	C	D	E	F	G	H	I	J	K	L
1												
2			Salary			Job Satisfaction			Opportunities for Promotion			
3	Weights		50			25			25			
4		Minimum	Most likely	Maximum	Minimum	Most likely	Maximum	Minimum	Most likely	Maximum		
5	Promotion	42,000	43,000	45,000	2	5	8	5	7	10		
6	New Employer	40,000	44,000	50,000	4	7	10	2	4	9		
7												
8												
9												
10												

Figure 10.16 Decision data for job.

Index

Note: Page numbers in *italic* and **bold** refers to figures and tables, respectively; Page numbers followed by "n" refer to footnotes.

Smart Decisions: A Structured Approach to Decision Analysis Using MCDA, First Edition.
Edited by Richard Edgar Hodgett, Sajid Siraj, and Ellen Louise Hogg.
© 2024 John Wiley & Sons Ltd. Published 2024 by John Wiley & Sons Ltd.